WALKING IN FREEDOM

REVISED & UPDATED

WALKING
in
FREEDOM

21 Days to Securing Your Identity in Christ

NEIL T. ANDERSON
& RICH MILLER

Regal

From Gospel Light
Ventura, California, U.S.A.

Published by Regal
From Gospel Light
Ventura, California, U.S.A.
www.regalbooks.com
Printed in the U.S.A.

First Edition, 1999
Second Edition, 2008

The Library of Congress has catalogued the first edition as follows:
Anderson, Neil T., 1942-
Walking in freedom / Neil T. Anderson and Rich Miller.
p. cm.
ISBN 0-8307-2394-3
1. Freedom (Theology)—Prayer-books and devotions—English.
I. Miller, Rich, 1954- . II. Title.
BT810.2.A57 1999
242'.2—dc21
98-32025
CIP

1 2 3 4 5 6 7 8 9 10 / 15 14 13 12 11 10 09 08

Rights for publishing this book outside the U.S.A. or in non-English languages are
administered by Gospel Light Worldwide, an international not-for-profit ministry.
For additional information, please visit www.glww.org, email info@glww.org, or write
to Gospel Light Worldwide, 1957 Eastman Avenue, Ventura, CA 93003, U.S.A.

CONTENTS

INTRODUCTION

God wants all His children to walk in the freedom Christ purchased for them at Calvary. In his letter to the Galatians, Paul wrote, "It was for freedom that Christ set us free; therefore keep standing firm and do not be subject again to a yoke of slavery" (Galatians 5:1).

This Scripture makes several things very clear:

1. Jesus Christ is the One who has already set us free from the slavery of sin.
2. Jesus set us free so that we can stand firm and walk in that freedom.
3. It is possible for us to lose in our experience the freedom Christ has given us.
4. God says it is our responsibility to stand firm and resist being enslaved again.

Every child of God has been given the responsibility to make right choices in life. We must choose truth, reject lies, forgive those who hurt us, flee temptation, and so on. But God did not leave us here as orphans to fend for ourselves. God Himself, in the Person of the Holy Spirit, has personally come to dwell in all believers. The Spirit alone gives us the power to walk in the freedom that is ours in Christ. He alone enables us to mature in Christ. Consider the following Scriptures:

But I say, walk by the Spirit, and you will not carry out the desire of the flesh (Galatians 5:16).

Now the Lord is the Spirit, and where the Spirit of the Lord is, there is liberty. But we all, with unveiled face beholding as in a mirror the glory of the Lord, are being transformed into the same image from glory to glory, just as from the Lord, the Spirit (2 Corinthians 3:17-18).

God's great desire for our lives is that we become more and more like the Lord Jesus Christ. We are radically changed (transformed) as we fix our eyes on our glorious Lord, empowered by the Spirit of liberty to have our minds renewed by the truth (see Romans 12:2).

This 21-day devotional guide is designed to reinforce the liberating work God has already begun in you. It will be most effective if you have recently walked through the Steps to Freedom in Christ (or the "Steps"). If you have not been through the Steps to Freedom in Christ, we encourage you to do so, preferably during your study of this devotional. The Steps appear at the end of this book for your use.

The Steps to Freedom in Christ is a practical guide to fulfilling James 4:7: "Submit therefore to God. Resist the devil and he will flee from you."

We submit to God by confessing and repenting of sin, forgiving those who have hurt us and humbly surrendering our lives to His Lordship. We resist the devil by rejecting his lies, choosing to believe the truth of God's Word and exercising our authority in Christ over the devil's influence in our lives. The Steps to Freedom in Christ will help you do just that.

A periodic, thorough spiritual housecleaning is healthy for every child of God. Proverbs 28:13-14 promises great blessing from God as we deal with the spiritual "garbage" in our lives, while warning of serious consequences if we don't:

He who conceals his sins does not prosper, but whoever confesses and renounces them finds mercy. Blessed is the man who always fears the LORD, but he who hardens his heart falls into trouble (*NIV*).

The Steps to Freedom in Christ are a thorough moral and spiritual inventory that will give you the opportunity to deeply repent of your sin and make the renewed choice to return to your first love, Jesus Christ.

Do you struggle with habitual sins, obsessive thoughts, nagging doubts, plaguing guilt and shame, fears, anger or confusion? Do you feel powerless against the temptations, accusations or lying deceptions of the enemy? Do you find it hard to live in humility and submission to God and others? The Steps to Freedom in Christ have been used of God to set hundreds of thousands of His precious children free in Christ.

Before you can maintain freedom in Christ, you may have to regain it. Once you do so, this *Walking in Freedom* devotional will be even more meaningful for you.

Each daily lesson in this guide will provide encouragement in the following areas:

- the truth about God
- the truth about you
- the truth about freedom

You will also find "Prayer for Today," an address to God that can serve as a springboard for your own time of talking with our Father. In addition, we have included a daily Scripture reading, which is a suggested chapter of the Bible for you to read during each of the 21 days. Finally, we have provided space for daily journaling, giving you a place to keep a record of what God is teaching you and doing in your life.

Seven times during this three-week devotional guide you will find a Freedom Refresher. These brief exercises each correspond to one of the seven Steps to Freedom in Christ. You will have the opportunity to let God bring to your mind additional issues in each area so that you can walk with God in even greater freedom in Christ!

This 21-day devotional concludes with an exercise entitled "Focal Point." This project will help you zero in on and focus your prayer attention on the most pressing spiritual needs in your life, even after completing this *Walking in Freedom* guide. As the Lord leads, you can also share your findings from "Focal Point" with other trustworthy believers who will pray for you in these areas.

We strongly urge you to complete the entire lesson for each day. We also encourage you to set aside time during 21 consecutive days to work through the entire guide. Jesus reminded us, "The thief comes only to steal and kill and destroy; I came that they might have life, and have it abundantly" (John 10:10).

Paying attention to the world, the flesh and the devil will keep you from walking in liberty. Jesus the Good Shepherd invites you to follow Him and enter His life of spiritual health and freedom.

You can expect the enemy of your soul to throw all kinds of distractions at you, both in your mind and in your circumstances. He will try to convince you that you don't need to bother completing this book, or he will push you to race through it. He will try to get you to give up pursuing the truth and instead give in to lies such as:

- This is too hard.
- I can't do this.
- This won't make any difference in my life.
- Skipping some sections won't matter.

Don't let him win the battle for your mind, no matter how intense the pressure might be. Claim 1 John 4:4 out loud as you begin:

[I am] from God, . . . and have overcome them; because greater is He who is in [me] than he who is in the world.

To encourage you in this three-week walk in freedom, we have included the following prayer for you to pray out loud:

Dear heavenly Father, Your Son, the Lord Jesus Christ, already purchased my freedom at the cross. You have also given me all I need to walk in that freedom through the Spirit of God, the Word of God and the people of God. In addition, You have given me Your armor by which I can stand firm against all the schemes of the devil and make responsible choices.

I choose right now, by Your grace and strength, Lord, to walk in the truth, righteousness and peace that are already mine in Christ. I reject all the lies, temptations, accusations and condemning fears of the devil.

I also choose to lift up the shield of faith, put on the helmet of salvation and take up the sword of the Spirit, which is the Word of God.

Heavenly Father, thank You that I have the sound mind of Christ and that my body is the temple of the Holy Spirit. Therefore I stand against all attempts of the enemy or my flesh to distract or discourage me. I ask You to enable me to concentrate on each lesson and persevere throughout the entire guide.

During these next three weeks, I ask that You please reveal to my mind all of the issues in my life that are hindering me from walking in freedom in Christ. I trust You to be my rock, my fortress and my deliverer. In Jesus' powerful, liberating name I pray. Amen.

As a step of faith, indicating your resolve to walk in freedom, no matter what the cost, please read and then sign the following commitment:

∽ *A Freedom Pledge* ∽

In the name and authority of the Lord Jesus Christ, and by His empowering Holy Spirit, I hereby commit myself to walking in freedom. I choose this _____ day of _____ in the year of our Lord _____ to do whatever it takes to walk with God in the light. As an expression of that commitment, I here and now resolve to undertake and complete this guide during the next 21 days. I trust in God's grace to enable me to do so.

I recognize that making and keeping this commitment in no way changes God's unconditional acceptance of me in Christ. This is simply a choice I am making of my own free will in order to take responsibility for my spiritual health and growth.

May the Lord alone be glorified through the completion of this guide and the resulting changes in my life.

Signed in the presence of my loving heavenly Father,

_____

A NEW LEASE ON LIFE

Congratulations! You have taken an important step toward maintaining your freedom in Christ by opening up this guide and turning to the first day's lesson. What a wonderful promise we have from God in James 4:8: "Draw near to God and He will draw near to you." Let's claim that promise in prayer as we begin:

Dear heavenly Father, thank You that I have a relationship with You through Jesus Christ. I am Your child. I choose to take time out now to be in Your holy, loving presence. Please open my ears to listen as a disciple. I look forward to our time together. In Jesus' name I pray. Amen.

The Truth About God

Jesus Christ, the eternal God in human flesh, made some incredible claims when He was here on earth. When His dear friend Lazarus had died and already been four days in the tomb, Jesus proclaimed to the dead man's sister Martha:

I am the resurrection and the life; he who believes in Me shall live even if he dies, and everyone who lives and believes in Me shall never die. Do you believe this? (John 11:25-26).

What an amazing statement! Jesus declared that He was not just the giver of life but life itself! He proved the truth of that claim shortly thereafter when He called out with a loud voice, "Lazarus, come forth" (v. 43). And Lazarus came forth; he had no choice! Do you realize that if Jesus had simply shouted, "Come forth," every dead person in every tomb in the entire world would have come out? What awesome power, what incredible authority—the right to give life! The apostle John recorded earlier in his Gospel the words of Jesus that confirm this fact:

> For just as the Father raises the dead and gives them life,
> even so the Son also gives life to whom He wishes (5:21).

Jesus called Himself "the bread of life" (6:35) who "came that they might have life, and might have it abundantly" (10:10). Peter referred to Him as "the Prince of life" (Acts 3:15). In his first letter, John described Jesus as "the Word of Life" (1 John 1:1).

Are you getting the message? There is simply no spiritual life (union of the human soul with God) apart from Jesus. He indeed is "the way, and the truth, and the life" (John 14:6). Where Jesus is, there is life; where Jesus is not, there is no life. It is as simple as that because Jesus is life itself!

The Truth About You

People without Jesus are people without eternal life. They may think they are living the good life or living life to the full, but they are deceived, blinded by Satan, the god of this world. The apostle Paul accurately described every unbeliever when he wrote:

> And you were dead in your trespasses and sins, in which
> you formerly walked according to the course of this
> world, according to the prince of the power of the air,

of the spirit that is now working in the sons of disobedience (Ephesians 2:1-2).

Apart from Christ, people are physically alive but spiritually dead—that is, separated from God, without the life of God in them. But praise God, things changed when we trusted in Jesus alone to save us! We have been born again by the Spirit of God (see John 3:1-8) so that now the following is true of us:

> But God, being rich in mercy, because of His great love with which He loved us, even when we were dead in our transgressions, made us alive together with Christ (by grace you have been saved) (Ephesians 2:4-5).

No matter what you may be going through today, for a moment lift up your eyes to the Giver of Life. Lift up your voice in praise to Him. For in Christ you are spiritually and eternally alive.

The Truth About Freedom

Are you trusting in Jesus Christ alone to save you, as a free gift of His grace? If so, you can have the complete assurance of your salvation today. Listen to John's words:

> And the testimony is this, that God has given us eternal life, and this life is in His Son. He who has the Son has the life; he who does not have the Son of God does not have the life. These things I have written to you who believe in the name of the Son of God, so that you may know that you have eternal life (1 John 5:11-13).

Did you catch John's words "so that you may know that you have eternal life"? Not "hope." Not "wonder." Not "look forward to when you die." But "*have*." Present tense! Now! What a relief!

For Christians there ought to be no fear of death, for we have eternal life! Don't believe tormenting thoughts of condemnation and hell.

> Therefore there is now no condemnation for those who are in Christ Jesus. For the law of the Spirit of life in Christ Jesus has set you free from the law of sin and of death (Romans 8:1-2).

Jesus came to set us free from the fear of death, as Hebrews 2:14-15 strongly proclaims:

> Therefore, since the children share in flesh and blood, He Himself [Jesus] likewise also partook of the same, that through death He might render powerless him who had the power of death, that is, the devil, and might free those who through fear of death were subject to slavery all their lives.

Prayer for Today

Dear heavenly Father, I thank You that You are the author of life and that Your Son is life. I thank You that I have eternal life in Him and that I shall never perish and that no one can snatch me out of His hand or Your hand [see John 10:27-30]. I choose today to renounce the fear of death and instead rejoice in the new life I have in Christ. I can never thank You enough for what Your Son, the Lord Jesus, went through to purchase my life with His shed blood. In Jesus' name I pray. Amen.

DAILY SCRIPTURE READING:
EPHESIANS 1

Daily Journal
*(personal reflections on what God has been
saying to me and doing in my life)*

_____
_____
_____
_____
_____
_____
_____
_____
_____
_____
_____
_____
_____
_____
_____
_____
_____
_____
_____
_____
_____
_____
_____
_____
_____

YOU'RE WELCOME!

When you come into someone's house, you know right away if that person is glad to see you or not. Believers who practice hospitality have a special way of putting you at ease and making you feel right at home. But where did that love of others come from? From the warmhearted God of the universe who wants us to know that in Christ we are welcomed into His heart and home with open arms. Let's begin today's lesson in prayer to our gracious, accepting, welcoming Father:

Dear heavenly Father, so often I view You as disapproving, impatient or irritated with me. At times, it is hard for me to understand Your grace, for this is not a gracious world in which I live. Please open my eyes to unconditional love and acceptance. I come to You as Your child. Help me to comprehend the kind of Father You are. In Jesus' name I pray. Amen.

The Truth About God

Grace. Most of us can rattle off the Christian textbook definition: "unmerited favor." I don't know about you, but that definition has about as much warmth as an IRS audit. But the Bible tells us that God is indeed gracious, or full of grace. Perhaps the Word of God can help us understand the truth of what that means. Consider the following Scripture verses:

The LORD is compassionate and gracious, slow to anger and abounding in lovingkindness. He will not always strive with us; nor will He keep His anger forever. He has not dealt with us according to our sins, nor rewarded us according to our iniquities (Psalm 103:8-10).

Therefore the LORD longs to be gracious to you, and therefore He waits on high to have compassion on you (Isaiah 30:18).

We cannot understand the depth of God's grace in accepting us into His presence through Jesus Christ unless we first understand the depth of our depravity before He saved us. The Bible uses these words to describe our condition apart from Christ: "lost," "helpless," "sinners," "hostile," "enemies," "wicked," "useless," "unrighteous," "ungodly," "without hope" and "children of wrath," among others. Not a pretty picture.

But the moment we put our trust in Him, in an instant, we were transformed into accepted, beloved children, adopted into the family of God. How? By absolutely nothing we did or could do, but by God's gracious, merciful heart. Read on:

For we also once were foolish ourselves, disobedient, deceived, enslaved to various lusts and pleasures, spending our life in malice and envy, hateful, hating one another. But when the kindness of God our Savior and His love for mankind appeared, He saved us, not on the basis of deeds which we have done in righteousness, but according to His mercy, by the washing of regeneration and renewing by the Holy Spirit, whom He poured out upon us richly through Jesus Christ our Savior, so that being justified by His grace we might be made heirs according to the hope of eternal life (Titus 3:3-7).

The Truth About You

So what does all this mean for you and me? Lots. The apostle Paul put it this way:

> Therefore, having been justified by faith, we have peace with God through our Lord Jesus Christ, through whom also we have obtained our introduction by faith into this grace in which we stand; and we exult in hope of the glory of God (Romans 5:1-2).

Through Jesus, then, we have been introduced to the grace of God. A grace in which we now stand and in which we will stand for all eternity! Just as God saved us by His grace (not by our religious performance), so He will continue to accept us by His grace all the days of our lives. He accepts us, includes us and receives us as His children whether our behavior is good, bad or ugly. He accepts us before we sin; He accepts us while we sin; He accepts us after we sin.

Does this sound too good to be true? Paul assures us that God's gracious, unconditional love and acceptance of us in Christ is both a present-day reality and a truth:

> In love He predestined us to adoption as sons through Jesus Christ to Himself, according to the kind intention of His will, to the praise of the glory of His grace, which He freely bestowed on us in the Beloved (Ephesians 1:4-6).

Paul continues in Ephesians to talk about God's lavishing His grace on us. Now, obviously, God does not delight in our sin. In fact, He hates it. But the reality of our sin does not negate the truth of God's continuous and unconditional acceptance of us in Christ. It is all by grace, amazing grace. Believe it today!

The Truth About Freedom

Most of us struggle at times with guilt and shame. Guilt is feeling bad for what we have done. Shame is feeling bad for who we are. The path to freedom is to understand that personal guilt and shame were defeated at the cross and in Jesus' resurrection. For Christ died not only for our *sins* (what we did) but also for our *sin* (who we were). If God says we are no longer guilty or shameful, shouldn't we accept ourselves the same way He has?

First Corinthians 6:9-11 gives us a good picture of the power of the grace of God to change our guilt and shame into glory:

> Or do you not know that the unrighteous will not inherit the kingdom of God? Do not be deceived; neither fornicators, nor idolaters, nor adulterers, nor effeminate, nor homosexuals, nor thieves, nor the covetous, nor drunkards, nor revilers, nor swindlers, shall inherit the kingdom of God. Such were some of you; but you were washed, but you were sanctified, but you were justified in the name of the Lord Jesus Christ and in the Spirit of our God.

Remember that God's view of you is spelled a-c-c-e-p-t, not e-x-c-e-p-t. Child of God, throw off the chains of guilt and shame today. In God's presence, you're welcome!

Prayer for Today

Dear heavenly Father, I praise You for the riches of Your grace that You have lavished on me in Christ Jesus. Your grace is glorious. I sit here and marvel at the truth that I am completely accepted and adopted into Your family. I am sorry for believing the slanderous accusations of the enemy that You are harsh and cruel or that I am guilty and shameful. I do believe Your Word; help me in my unbelief [see Mark 9:24]. Cause the truth to filter down into the very depth of my soul so that I can live to the glory of Your grace. In Jesus' gracious name I pray. Amen.

DAILY SCRIPTURE READING:
EPHESIANS 2

Daily Journal

_____
_____
_____
_____
_____
_____
_____
_____
_____
_____
_____
_____
_____
_____
_____
_____
_____
_____
_____
_____
_____
_____
_____
_____
_____
_____

_____

_____

_____

_____

_____

_____

_____

_____

_____

_____

_____

_____

_____

_____

_____

_____

_____

_____

_____

_____

_____

_____

_____

_____

_____

_____

_____

_____

A CLEAN SLATE

If you were to select an animal to depict God's character, which one would you choose? A lion? A tiger maybe? An eagle perhaps? How about a lamb?

Even though Jesus is called the Lion of the tribe of Judah in Revelation 5:5 (a fulfillment of the messianic prophecy of Genesis 49:9-10), He is referred to as the Lamb 26 times in that last book of the Bible. When John the Baptist spotted Him, he cried out, "Behold, the Lamb of God who takes away the sin of the world!" (John 1:29).

The significance of this name of Jesus is so critical that we need God's enabling to understand it. Let's pray:

Dear Father, it is so clear that Your ways and thoughts are far higher than mine. Your judgments are unsearchable and Your ways beyond my comprehension. Please graciously open my eyes, heart and mind to see and understand the life-changing truth that You are indeed the Lamb of God who takes away my sins. In Jesus' name I pray. Amen.

The Truth About God

When Israel was preparing for the exodus from Egypt, each family was told to kill a one-year-old unblemished male lamb. They smeared some of the blood of that lamb around the outside door to their home. God promised that the angel that night would "pass over" that house and spare the firstborn child within from death (see Exodus 12:13). The blood of the lamb accomplished this protection.

Once the system of sacrifices for sins was set up in Israel, the high priest would make atonement for the sins of the nation once a year. The blood of the sacrifice, sprinkled on the mercy seat of the Ark of the Covenant inside the Most Holy Place, would serve to cover the sins of the nation for another year.

Isaiah prophesied that another Lamb would come. Today we know that Lamb as the Messiah, Jesus Christ. Feast your eyes on some of Isaiah's incredible words:

> But He was pierced through for our transgressions, He was crushed for our iniquities; the chastening for our well-being fell upon Him, and by His scourging we are healed. All of us like sheep have gone astray, each of us has turned to his own way; but the LORD has caused the iniquity of us all to fall on Him. He was oppressed and He was afflicted, yet He did not open His mouth; like a lamb that is led to slaughter, and like a sheep that is silent before its shearers, so He did not open His mouth (Isaiah 53:5-7).

At the Passover, a lamb was slain and its blood protected a family. On the Day of Atonement, the blood of the sacrifice covered the sins of a nation. But now the Lamb of God who takes away the sins of the world has come—the gentle, humble Jesus. Praise His name!

> He came as High Priest of this better system which we now have. He went into that greater, perfect tabernacle in heaven, not made by men nor part of this world, and once for all took blood into that inner room, the Holy of Holies, and sprinkled it on the mercy seat; but it was

not the blood of goats and calves. No, he took his own blood, and with it he, by himself, made sure of our eternal salvation (Hebrews 9:11-12, *TLB*).

The Truth About You

Because of our faith in the sinless sacrifice of the Lamb of God, we are forgiven of all our sins—past, present and future! Christ paid the debt we owed to God. "Where there is forgiveness of these things, there is no longer any offering for sin" (Hebrews 10:18). There is absolutely nothing we can do to add to the finished work of Christ on the cross. He cried out, "It is finished!" (John 19:30) or, literally, "Paid in full." All that is left is for us to receive by faith the truth that we are clean. Let the following words of truth penetrate your heart:

> As far as the east is from the west, so far has He removed our transgressions from us (Psalm 103:12).

> Though your sins are as scarlet, they will be as white as snow; though they are red like crimson, they will be like wool (Isaiah 1:18).

> Who is a God like you, who pardons sin and forgives the transgression of the remnant of his inheritance? You do not stay angry forever but delight to show mercy. You will again have compassion on us; you will tread our sins underfoot and hurl all our iniquities into the depths of the sea (Micah 7:18-19, *NIV*).

> In Him we have redemption through His blood, the forgiveness of our trespasses, according to the riches of His grace which He lavished on us (Ephesians 1:7-8).

> And their sins and their lawless deeds I will remember no more (Hebrews 10:17).

Do you believe it? God wants you to know that in Christ your sins are forgiven. The debt is paid. The past is behind you. The slate is clean. Praise His glorious name!

The Truth About Freedom

The most natural response to knowing you are forgiven is to worship the Lamb who bought you that forgiveness. In Revelation 4 and 5, a growing crescendo of praise to God the Father and Jesus the Son climaxes with all creation in worship. We encourage you to read that whole section of Scripture, but for now why not join in on the chorus:

> You are worthy to take the scroll and to open its seals, because you were slain, and with your blood you purchased men for God from every tribe and language and people and nation. You have made them to be a kingdom and priests to serve our God, and they will reign on the earth. . . . Worthy is the Lamb, who was slain, to receive power and wealth and wisdom and strength and honor and glory and praise! . . . To him who sits on the throne and to the Lamb be praise and honor and glory and power, for ever and ever! (Revelation 5:9-13, *NIV*).

At the conclusion of this outburst of praise, "The four living creatures said, 'Amen,' and the elders fell down and worshiped" (v. 14, *NIV*). How can we not do the same?

Prayer for Today

Dear heavenly Father, I worship You and the Lamb of God who takes away the sins of the world. To know that the way into Your throne room, the Most Holy Place, is open to me is incredible. What the high priest could only do once a year, I can do 24 hours a day, 7 days a week. Thank You! Thank You that I am truly forgiven and cleansed through the blood of Christ. I glorify Your name and offer up this praise and thanksgiving in Jesus' name. Amen.

DAILY SCRIPTURE READING:
EPHESIANS 3

Daily Journal

_____
_____
_____
_____
_____
_____
_____
_____
_____
_____
_____
_____
_____
_____
_____
_____
_____
_____
_____
_____
_____
_____

FREEDOM
REFRESHER
={ ONE }=

It is very common, even after thoroughly walking through the Steps to Freedom in Christ, to find the Lord bringing additional things to your mind that you still need to resolve. This in no way invalidates the reality of what He has already done in your life. It is actually a healthy sign that you are remaining open to His leading and cleansing. God knows how much we can handle at any given moment, so He very often brings us the experience of freedom in stages, like the peeling of layers on an onion.

In this first Freedom Refresher, we will give the Lord the opportunity to bring to your mind any additional trouble spots in your life that relate to Step One in the Steps to Freedom in Christ. If you want to do a more complete spiritual housecleaning than we are able to perform here, feel free to go back through the complete version of Step One (or all the Steps, for that matter) instead. The Steps to Freedom in Christ can be found at the back of this book.

You may recall that Step One focuses on past or present involvement with any occult, cult or false religious beliefs or practices. Be especially sensitive to the Lord as He may bring to your mind any books, movies, magazines, video or computer games, TV shows or music you were involved with that you need to renounce. Media that glorify Satan or are gruesomely violent, erotic or frightening ought to have no place in a believer's life. We encourage you to pray out loud the following prayer:

Dear heavenly Father, I ask You to bring to my mind anything and everything I have done knowingly or unknowingly that involves occult, cult or non-Christian teachings or practices. Remind me of any music, written material, movies or games that I listened to, viewed or played that are contrary to Your truth. Enable me to recall any non-Christian pacts, pledges or vows that I have made and all satanic lies that I have believed. I want to experience Your freedom by renouncing them. In Jesus' name I pray. Amen.

If you are certain you have previously confessed aloud and renounced something, you don't need to do so again (unless you have subsequently participated in it). For each thing the Lord brings to mind, pray the following prayer out loud from your heart.

Dear Lord, I confess that I have participated in [name the specific belief, practice and/or thing]. I know that it was evil and offensive in Your sight. Thank You for Your forgiveness. I renounce any and all involvement with [name the belief, practice and/or thing], and I take back any and all ground the enemy gained in my life through this activity. In Jesus' name I pray. Amen.

Do any objects (occult paraphernalia, books, CDs, DVDs, amulets, objects of superstition or false worship, and so forth) still remain in your possession? These very easily could still tie you to those evil practices. Let the Lord speak to you now about these items, and be obedient to destroy anything He directs you to dispose of. Do this no matter how valuable (in terms of money or sentimental meaning) this item may be to you.

Great blessing and a new level of freedom will come from such an act of obedience. Look up Acts 19:11-20 (especially verses 18-20) for a biblical example of just such an act of repentance.

HOLY, HOLY, HOLY!

Some people have come to believe a rather tame, manageable view of God. To some extent, this is the Church's fault. In our efforts to encourage people not to see God as some sort of distant and aloof taskmaster, we may have at times gone too far. Too many people, Christians included, have lost the sense of the holiness of God and have a poor understanding of what the Bible means about fearing Him. This anemic view of God has, in large part, left the Church carelessly and dangerously tolerant of sin.

The revelation of Scripture, however, makes it clear that the most striking attribute of God, the one characteristic of Him that arrests the attention of those that see Him, is that He is holy. We must return to a biblical understanding of the holiness of God. Let us pray toward that end:

> *Most holy heavenly Father, though You have graciously made Yourself approachable to us through Jesus Christ, You remain high and lifted up and holy in all Your ways. Were we to see You as You really are, we would fall on our faces in adoration and praise. Open our eyes to the reality of who You are and teach us to revere You. In Jesus' holy name I pray. Amen.*

The Truth About God

In describing Jesus' work as the ultimate High Priest who paid for our sins by His blood, the book of Hebrews gives a good description of His holiness:

For it was fitting for us to have such a high priest, holy, innocent, undefiled, separated from sinners and exalted above the heavens (7:26).

The holiness of God refers to His utter separation from all that is evil or impure, to such an extent that He cannot even be tempted to do evil (see James 1:13). He is not simply pure; He is purity itself. He is the standard by which everything else is measured. He is high and exalted in moral character beyond our comprehension. Isaiah 6:1-3 gives us a glimpse of God's awesome, exalted holiness:

> In the year of King Uzziah's death, I saw the Lord sitting on a throne, lofty and exalted, with the train of His robe filling the temple. Seraphim stood above Him, each having six wings: with two he covered his face, and with two he covered his feet, and with two he flew. And one called out to another and said, "Holy, Holy, Holy, is the LORD of hosts, the whole earth is full of His glory."

Isaiah cried out in despair at this vision, fearing that he was a dead man for having looked upon the Holy One. God, in His mercy, touched Isaiah's mouth, cleansed him of his sins and called him into service to be a holy mouthpiece for God.

John the apostle fainted in fear at the sight of the resurrected and exalted Christ in Revelation 1. Jesus graciously touched him and told him not to be afraid. Then He proceeded to unveil to His servant the most sweeping prophetic vision in all Scripture.

Why did these godly men react in this way? Because they saw God as He really is—and He is holy.

The Truth About You

If we were brought face to face with the purity of God's holiness, we would immediately be aware of our own sin. Apart from

Christ, we are sinful people, wrapped up in ourselves and filled with unbelief.

In Luke 5, Peter reluctantly followed Jesus' instruction to try fishing again in deep water, despite having spent the entire night fishing with no success. When he saw the boats sinking with the catch they pulled in, he cried out, "Go away from me, Lord, for I am a sinful man!" (Luke 5:8).

The knowledge of the Holy One does that to us. A clear vision of His awesome purity brings us to our knees in repentance from our sinful ways. That is a healthy response to knowing God.

Despite the reality that we so often give in to sin, the Bible makes clear that we are not sinners. In fact, the very opposite is true. At least 60 times in the New Testament alone, believers in Christ are called saints. This is the second truth that is brought to bear upon our hearts in view of the holiness of God. Though we are not yet perfected in holiness, we are of His divine nature (see 2 Peter 1:4). Yes, in our core nature and identity (who we are in the inner man), we are holy ones, or saints. Skeptical? Let's allow the Word of God to speak for itself:

> Paul, called as an apostle, . . . to the church of God which is at Corinth, to those who have been sanctified in Christ Jesus, saints by calling (1 Corinthians 1:1-2).

> Do you not know that you are a temple of God and that the Spirit of God dwells in you? If any man destroys the temple of God, God will destroy him, for the temple of God is holy, and that is what you are (1 Corinthians 3:16-17).

> So, as those who have been chosen of God, holy and beloved (Colossians 3:12).

It is significant that Paul uses the term "saints" (holy ones) to describe the Corinthians. Notice he says they are "saints by calling," though he spends a good portion of the rest of that book reproving them for their unsaintly behavior.

That is where our confusion often lies. Because we sin, we consider ourselves to be sinners and assume God does, too. He says in His Word that we are not sinners but saints who still have the capacity to sin. This is good news, because a saint can live righteously, but a sinner cannot.

The Truth About Freedom

In essence, living free in Christ means living according to who we really are as children of God. When our behavior as Christians lines up with our identity as holy ones (saints) filled with the Holy Spirit, we experience freedom. When we live a fleshly, or worldly, identity instead, we get trapped in sin. Paul's second letter to the Corinthians reveals this truth:

> For we are the temple of the living God; just as God said, "I will dwell in them and walk among them; and I will be their God, and they shall be My people. Therefore, come out from their midst and be separate," says the Lord. "And do not touch what is unclean; and I will welcome you. And I will be a father to you, and you shall be sons and daughters to Me," says the Lord Almighty. Therefore, having these promises, beloved, let us cleanse ourselves from all defilement of flesh and spirit, perfecting holiness in the fear of God (2 Corinthians 6:16–7:1).

We fear God the Lord when we live with the conscious awareness of an all-knowing, everywhere-present and holy God. Our fear springs from a deep reverential awe of Him, resulting in a life that hates sin and loves righteousness. This life is the pursuit of holiness, seeking to work out the salvation that God has already worked in us (see Philippians 2:12-13) through the enabling power of the Holy Spirit. It is the life of a saint. It is the life of freedom.

Prayer for Today

Dear heavenly Father, I praise You for Your matchless grace and for the purity of Your holiness. I stand in awe of You and Your Word, which calls me to be holy as You are holy. I love Your Word, for it is "living and active and sharper than any two-edged sword" [Hebrews 4:12]. Only by Your Holy Spirit's filling can I walk in holiness before You. I thank You that You have changed my very nature so that I am indeed a saint, a holy one, set apart from sin for worship and service to You. I bless You and pray in Jesus' name. Amen.

DAILY SCRIPTURE READING:
EPHESIANS 4

Daily Journal

_____

_____

_____

_____

_____

_____

_____

_____

_____

_____

_____

5

THE REAL THING

The prayer the apostle Paul prayed for the Ephesian believers provides a great model for us today. For just as we need our heart eyes enlightened to the holiness of God, so also we need to clearly see the love of God. Let's pray, according to Ephesians 3:16-19:

> *Dear heavenly Father, I pray that You would grant me, according to the riches of Your glory, to be strengthened with power through Your Spirit in the inner man so that Christ may dwell in my heart through faith; and that I, being rooted and grounded in love, may be able to comprehend with all the saints what is the breadth and length and height and depth, and to know the love of Christ which surpasses knowledge, that I may be filled up to all the fullness of God. In Jesus' name I pray. Amen.*

The Truth About God

"God is love." You've heard it, said it and thought it, probably hundreds if not thousands of times. Even the secular world wants to believe that God is love. It has become almost a cliché in our culture. Truthfully, God *is* love according to 1 John 4:8. It is His nature to love, and we have become a partaker of that same nature.

> By this the love of God was manifested in us, that God has sent His only begotten Son into the world so that we might live through Him (v. 9).

Recall John 3:16: "For God so loved the world, that He gave His only begotten Son." The love of God is manifested in giving. Because God loves, He gives; and God's love is supremely demonstrated in the sacrificial giving and sending of Jesus, His only Son, who came to live and die for the sins of the whole world.

Every time you doubt that God is love, take another look at Jesus and His death on the cross. There, once and for all, God settled the question of His loving heart. "God demonstrates His own love toward us, in that while we were yet sinners, Christ died for us" (Romans 5:8). He proved beyond a shadow of a doubt that He is love.

Paul reveals what the character of God is like in the "Love Chapter," 1 Corinthians 13. Understand that the love of God is the ultimate fulfillment of these qualities:

Love is patient, love is kind. It does not envy, it does not boast, it is not proud. It is not rude, it is not self-seeking, it is not easily angered, it keeps no record of wrongs. Love does not delight in evil but rejoices with the truth. It always protects, always trusts, always hopes, always perseveres. Love never fails (vv. 4-8, *NIV*).

In a world of increasing hostility, anger, impatience, rudeness and hate, we need a refuge from all the harshness and cruelty. You may find a measure of comfort in the love of some people. But you will find perfect love in God—all the time. For *God is love*.

The Truth About You

How much does God love us? Notice what Jesus had to say on two occasions in the Gospel of John:

Just as the Father has loved Me, I have also loved you; abide in My love (15:9).

I in them and you in me. May they be brought to complete unity to let the world know that you sent me and have loved them even as you have loved me (17:23, *NIV*).

Did you catch that? Did you really understand what Jesus said? He wanted us to know that the love God has for Jesus is the very same love the Father and Son have for us. Incredible! An eternal, perfect, unfailing love constantly pulses from the heart of God toward you and me.

Let these healing words from Andrew Murray's book *Abide in Christ* wash over your soul:

As one of His redeemed ones, you are His delight, and all His desire is to you, with the longing of a love which is stronger than death, and which many waters cannot quench. His heart yearns after you, seeking your fellowship and your love. Were it needed, He could die again to possess you. As the Father loved the Son, and could not live without Him, could not be God the blessed without Him—so Jesus loves you. His life is bound up in yours; you are to Him inexpressibly more indispensable and precious than you ever can know. You are one with Himself. "As the Father hath loved me, so I have loved you." What a love![1]

Finally, will God ever quit loving us? Paul laid that fear to rest when he wrote:

For I am convinced that neither death nor life, neither angels nor demons, neither the present nor the future, nor any powers, neither height nor depth, nor anything else in all creation, will be able to separate us from the love of God that is in Christ Jesus our Lord (Romans 8:38-39, *NIV*).

The Truth About Freedom

To walk in God's love is to walk in obedience to Him (see John 14:15; 15:10). Despite what the enemy would want us to believe, God's commandments are not burdensome (see 1 John 5:3). In fact, obedience to them is the only way to experience the fullness of joy in Christ (see John 15:11).

At times, however, we are not free to abandon ourselves to doing the will of God, because we are afraid of God and what He will do to us or with us. First John 4:18 says, however:

There is no fear in love; but perfect love casts out fear, because fear involves punishment, and the one who fears is not perfected in love.

As we saw in the last devotion, a healthy fear of God is the beginning of wisdom and knowledge and is a deterrent to doing evil. It is not healthy, though, to have a cringing, cowering fear or suspicious mistrust of your heavenly Father. Once you come to know the fullness of God's love, your reluctance to trust and obey Him melts away with the assurance of His genuine care for you. Do you trust Him today? Will you do what He says? It is the only path to freedom.

Prayer for Today
(A Prayer of Confession)

Dear heavenly Father, I confess that I have been afraid to let You have control of [name the area]. I recognize now that I have been deceived into thinking I could not trust You. Right now, by faith, I turn [name the area] over to You, my loving Father. Your love has won me over. I can rest in Your sheltering, strong arms and let all fear melt away from me like ice under a warm sun.

Thank You for forgiving me for all the doubts and fears I've had toward You. Many times I have felt like nobody could or would ever sincerely love me. But I thank You for the free-dom that comes from resting in and trusting in Your love. Enable me to grasp how broad and high and deep it is so that I can be filled to all Your fullness. In the name of my loving Lord and best friend, Jesus, I pray. Amen.

DAILY SCRIPTURE READING:
EPHESIANS 5

Daily Journal

_____
_____
_____
_____
_____
_____
_____
_____
_____
_____
_____
_____
_____
_____
_____
_____
_____
_____
_____
_____
_____

_____
_____
_____
_____
_____
_____
_____
_____
_____
_____
_____
_____
_____
_____
_____
_____
_____
_____
_____
_____
_____
_____
_____
_____
_____
_____
_____

Note

1. Andrew Murray, *Abide in Christ* (New Kensington, PA: Whitaker House, 1979), p. 142.

6

FREE AT LAST!

What does it mean to be free in Christ? In essence, being free in Christ means being delivered from the control of anything or anyone whose influence is at cross-purposes with God.

Satan, our sinful flesh within and the ungodly world without are all seeking to gain influence over us. What has Christ done to set us free from their power? What is our responsibility in walking in that freedom? These are critical matters for us to understand, lest we find ourselves staggering under a yoke of slavery once again. Let's pray for God's clear insight to know the truth:

Dear heavenly Father, I thank You for the joy and peace that come from experiencing freedom in Christ. I praise You for Your power and grace that have loosed the chains that held me captive to sin. How can I walk even more fully in the freedom for which You set me free? Open the eyes of my understanding, that I might see clearly the liberating work of Jesus Christ. And it's in His name I pray. Amen.

The Truth About God

The problem with most people is that they don't realize they are in bondage, so they don't see their need to be set free. Or if they do see their need, they believe the answer lies in some sort of self-help program of learning to cope with their problem or addiction. But the Bible tells us that apart from Christ, we are "foolish . . . disobedient, deceived, enslaved to various lusts and pleasures" (Titus 3:3). We don't need someone to come along and teach us how to cope better as slaves; we need someone to buy us out of slavery and set us free! We need the Redeemer, God Himself.

The book of Isaiah frequently identifies God as our Redeemer. The following are just two examples:

> But now, thus says the LORD, your Creator, O Jacob, and He who formed you, O Israel, "Do not fear, for I have redeemed you; I have called you by name; you are Mine!" (Isaiah 43:1).

> For your husband is your Maker, whose name is the LORD of hosts; and your Redeemer is the Holy One of Israel, who is called the God of all the earth (Isaiah 54:5).

In the book of Exodus, God declared, "I have surely seen the affliction of My people who are in Egypt, and have given heed to their cry because of their taskmasters, for I am aware of their sufferings" (3:7). So He promised Moses, "I am the LORD, and I will bring you out from under the burdens of the Egyptians, and I will deliver you from their bondage. I will also redeem you with an outstretched arm and with great judgments" (6:6).

The awful bondage and helplessness the Israelites experienced in Egypt are a picture of every human being's slavery to sin. In the Old Testament, God redeemed Israel (brought her out of slavery) through the deliverer Moses. In the New Testament, God personally came to earth through Christ to redeem us from the power of sin. The purchase price for humankind's freedom was His very own blood, the precious blood of Jesus. He is worthy of our praise!

You are worthy to take the scroll, and to open its seals; for You were slain, and have redeemed us to God by Your blood out of every tribe and tongue and people and nation, and have made us kings and priests to our God; and we shall reign on the earth (Revelation 5:9-10, *NKJV*).

The Truth About You

When you purchase something at a store, that item becomes legally yours. Because you paid for it, the store has no right to continue to claim ownership of it. It belongs to you. You possess it.

In the same way, because God redeemed us to Himself through Christ, we belong to Him. We are not our own, free to do whatever we please. That may, at first glance, seem like bad news. But it is not. We belong to a loving, caring heavenly Father who paid the ultimate price to make us His own. He can be trusted. First Corinthians 6:19-20 makes it clear whose we are and the right to ownership that God has over us:

Or do you not know that your body is a temple of the Holy Spirit who is in you, whom you have from God, and that you are not your own? For you have been bought with a price: therefore glorify God in your body.

In addition, the devil may try to convince us that we are still slaves to sin and under its control. But we are not! Read the following Scripture and rejoice:

But thanks be to God that though you were slaves of sin, you became obedient from the heart to that form of teaching to which you were committed, and having been freed from sin, you became slaves of righteousness (Romans 6:17-18).

Can we still be tempted to sin? Of course. Can we make the choice to give in to that temptation and commit sin? Yes. But do we have to give in to sin's seduction? Absolutely not! We are truly free to choose righteousness, because we are "dead to sin, but alive to God in Christ Jesus" (Romans 6:11).

The Truth About Freedom

"Glorify God in your body." That is what 1 Corinthians 6:20 says, and it is a huge key to freedom. How are you using your mind, hands, mouth, feet, eyes, ears, sexual organs, and so forth? Are they tools in the hands of God for His glory, or are they instruments for sin? How you answer those questions is critical. Romans 6:11-13 shows us the way to freedom:

> Even so consider yourselves to be dead to sin, but alive to God in Christ Jesus. Therefore do not let sin reign in your mortal body so that you obey its lusts, and do not go on presenting the members of your body to sin as instruments of unrighteousness; but present yourselves to God as those alive from the dead, and your members as instruments of righteousness to God.

What a sad thing that so many Christians who have been bought out of slavery to sin by the blood of the Lord Jesus Christ are still needlessly in bondage! Christian, don't obey the lying lusts of your sinful flesh. Sin never delivers what it promises. Though it may bring gratification for a moment, it can never bring the satisfaction of righteousness (see Matthew 5:6). Won't you make the decision today to present your entire body to God as an instrument of righteousness? Nothing in this world or in the flesh can deliver the peace of mind, clear conscience and joyful heart that freedom in Christ brings!

Prayer for Today

Dear heavenly Father, I realize now that my life is not my own. And though at first that seemed like bad news, I realize now that it's the best news I could hear! If I were left here on earth to fend for myself, I would surely perish. But knowing that I belong to You and that You are taking care of me brings me great security. In addition, thank You for redeeming me from my slavery to sin. I thank You that sin is no longer my master, for I am no longer "under law but under grace" [Romans 6:14]. I make the choice today to glorify You in my body by presenting my body and all its parts to You for doing what is right and good. I trust Your Spirit to empower me to live in this way. In Jesus' name I pray. Amen.

DAILY SCRIPTURE READING:
EPHESIANS 6

Daily Journal

_____

_____

_____

_____

_____

_____

_____

_____

_____

_____

_____

FREEDOM REFRESHER
{TWO}

To deceive means to "make (a person) believe what is not true; delude; mislead." Although we are Christ's sheep and Jesus is our Good Shepherd, it is easy for us to have "the wool pulled over our eyes." The devil's native tongue is deception, and we live in a world in which that language is spoken fluently.

This second Freedom Refresher corresponds to Step Two of the Steps to Freedom in Christ (see the back of this book), which is "Deception vs. Truth." The following prayer is a recommitment of the heart to walk in the light of God's truth:

Dear heavenly Father, I know that You want me to know the truth, believe the truth, speak the truth and live in accordance with the truth. Thank You that it is Your truth that will set me free.

I have trusted in Jesus alone to save me, so I know I am Your forgiven and accepted child. Therefore, because You accept me just as I am in Christ, I can be free to face my sin and not deny it, excuse it, tolerate it or blame others for it. I ask for the Holy Spirit to guide me into all truth and expose every way in which I have been deceived by the world, the flesh or the devil. In the name of Jesus, the Truth, I pray. Amen.

The difficulty in recognizing deception at work in our lives is fairly obvious. If we are being deceived, we are not aware that it is happening. This is the very nature of deception. The material in Step Two is very helpful in diagnosing potential areas of deception by the world, areas of self-deception, and wrong ways we defend ourselves. We also urge you to prayerfully consider the following questions. For any areas in which the Holy Spirit prompts you to admit you are being deceived, we heartily encourage you to pray through the prayer of confession at the end of this exercise.

1. Are there any areas of your life in which the Lord has been trying to caution or warn you about, but you have dismissed His counsel?

2. Are there any areas of your life in which close friends or family have pointed out concerns but you have denied that anything is wrong (though deep down you know they are right)?

3. Are you engaging in any practices (including email or cell-phone relationships) that you are keeping hidden from family and/or friends? Are you experiencing shame?

4. Are you finding your desire to walk with Christ, read God's Word, pray or have fellowship with other believers growing stagnant or cold? Is your heart growing harder?

5. Do you feel justified in harboring angry, bitter or lustful attitudes?

6. Are you isolating yourself from other Christians or keeping your relationships intentionally superficial?

For any deception that the Lord has revealed to your heart, pray the following prayer out loud:

Dear Lord, I confess that I have been deceived by [name the specific cause of deception]. I thank You for Your forgiveness, and I commit myself to walk only in Your truth. In Jesus' name I pray. Amen.

IN GOOD HANDS

The Christian life is a life of faith. In fact, "without faith it is impossible to please [God]" (Hebrews 11:6). Even though we cannot see God, His nature and ways have been revealed to us in His Word. Since we very often walk by sight and not by faith, it is easy to become overwhelmed by the circumstances of life around us and lose "sight" of God.

Fortunately, the Bible gives us great assurance that our God can be trusted. We can lean on Him and depend on Him, knowing that He will never change nor leave or forsake us. Are you struggling with believing that today? Let's ask God to refresh us with a renewed vision of who He is so that we can walk by faith in Him:

> *Dear heavenly Father, I must confess that in my life I struggle with trusting You, especially when times get tough. It is easy to lean on my own understanding rather than acknowledge You. Lord, I believe; help my unbelief! Reveal Yourself and Your ways to me so that I can follow You with my whole heart. In Jesus' name I pray. Amen.*

The Truth About God

One of the most encouraging aspects of God's character is that He is faithful. In essence, this means He always does what He says He will do. He is the first and greatest Promise Keeper! Throughout Scripture, God's great faithfulness is proclaimed, usually by people who went through the toughest trials of life. Consider the Scripture verses below; you will profit greatly from committing at least one of them to memory:

> The steps of a man are established by the LORD; and He delights in his way. When he falls, he will not be hurled headlong, because the LORD is the One who holds his hand. I have been young and now I am old, yet I have not seen the righteous forsaken, or his descendants begging bread (Psalm 37:23-25).

> Remember my affliction and my wandering, the wormwood and bitterness. Surely my soul remembers, and is bowed down within me. This I recall to my mind, therefore I have hope. The LORD's lovingkindnesses indeed never cease, for His compassions never fail. They are new every morning; great is Your faithfulness (Lamentations 3:19-23).

> No temptation has overtaken you but such as is common to man; and God is faithful, who will not allow you to be tempted beyond what you are able, but with the temptation will provide the way of escape also, so that you will be able to endure it (1 Corinthians 10:13).

> But the Lord is faithful, and He will strengthen and protect you from the evil one (2 Thessalonians 3:3).

These verses were written by three of the greatest veterans of the faith: David, Jeremiah and Paul. They did not live in luxury and ease but suffered some of the most intense physical, mental, emotional and spiritual agony known to humankind.

Yet consistently their testimonies resound with the cry, "God is faithful!"

Before you move on, take a moment to thank God for the various ways He has shown Himself to be faithful to you.

The Truth About You

Children are not responsible for making sure Mom and Dad will take care of them. It is the parents' responsibility to provide a safe and secure home where the children know their needs will be met. The children are then free to enjoy life as they grow and mature, knowing they will be well taken care of.

Are you anxious about your life? Are you losing sleep, wondering if you will be able to make it spiritually? Are you tempted to fret about financial or relational problems? Let's examine the words of Jesus and allow Him to calm our frazzled nerves and worried hearts:

> No one can serve two masters; for either he will hate the one and love the other, or he will be devoted to one and despise the other. You cannot serve God and wealth. For this reason I say to you, do not be worried about your life, as to what you will eat or what you will drink; nor for your body, as to what you will put on. Is not life more than food, and the body more than clothing? Look at the birds of the air, that they do not sow, nor reap nor gather into barns, and yet your heavenly Father feeds them. *Are you not worth much more than they?* And who of you by being worried can add a single hour to his life? And why are you worried about clothing? Observe how the lilies of the field grow; they do not toil nor do they spin, yet I say to you that not even Solomon in all his glory clothed himself like one of these. But if God so clothes the grass of the field, which is alive today and

tomorrow is thrown into the furnace, will He not much more clothe you? You of little faith! (Matthew 6:24-30, emphasis added).

Jesus' line of reasoning is clear: If God takes care of the birds and flowers, can't He be trusted to take care of us? The answer to that question is an obvious and unequivocal YES! We are God's redeemed children, of infinitely more value than animals and plants. He didn't go to the cross for them, but He did for you and me. "You were not redeemed with perishable things like silver or gold from your futile way of life inherited from your forefathers, but with precious blood, as of a lamb unblemished and spotless, the blood of Christ" (1 Peter 1:18-19).

The Truth About Freedom

Scripture admonishes us to cast all our anxieties (cares) on God, because He cares for us (see 1 Peter 5:7). Things we worry about don't determine who we are. Give everything that concerns you over to Him in prayer. Thank Him for His faithfulness. God promises to restore the wonderful gift of peace to you, peace that will guard your heart and mind in Christ Jesus (see Philippians 4:6-7). God wants you to be free from the hurry and worry of life even now. Praise the Lord!

Knowing that God is faithful to take care of us should prompt us to seek Him to meet our needs rather than worry about money or the material things we need. Consider again the words of Jesus:

Do not worry then, saying, "What will we eat?" or "What will we drink?" or "What will we wear for clothing?" For the Gentiles eagerly seek all these things; for your heavenly Father knows that you need all these things. But seek first His kingdom and His righteousness, and all these things shall be added to you. So do not worry about tomorrow; for tomorrow will care for itself. Each day has enough trouble of its own (Matthew 6:31-34).

Prayer for Today

Faithful Father, the more I look around me, the more I see Your hand of faithfulness at work. I thank You for the food and drink You give me each day, the clothes I have to wear and the shelter in which I live. Thank You for the people in my life who love me. Thank You for the money You provide to pay bills and meet the needs of my loved ones. But I choose this day not to put my trust in any of these things or people. The only guarantee I have each day is that You will still be there, and You will be faithful. I seek Your kingdom and Your righteousness first, and I choose not to be anxious for tomorrow. In Jesus' name I pray. Amen.

DAILY SCRIPTURE READING:
ROMANS 1

Daily Journal

_____

_____

_____

_____

_____

_____

_____

_____

8

NOTHING BUT THE TRUTH

Truth and trust go together. It is hard to trust someone who does not tell the truth. We have good reason to question many in authority, to doubt the truthfulness of their words, the sincerity of their motives and the genuineness of their character.

We are living in days that reflect the words of the prophet Isaiah: "Justice is turned back, and righteousness stands far away; for truth has stumbled in the street, and uprightness cannot enter. Yes, truth is lacking; and he who turns aside from evil makes himself a prey" (Isaiah 59:14-15). God stands in contrast to this rising tide of lies and deception in our world. We desperately need to know Him as the God of truth because Jesus said that knowing the truth sets us free. Let's pray:

Dear heavenly Father, it is easy to become jaded, skeptical and even cynical toward anyone who claims to be telling the truth, because lying is so commonplace. Remove any blinders from my eyes that keep me from seeing that You are the Truth, and that You always tell the truth. I need a firm foundation of truth in my life if I am to walk in freedom. In Jesus' name I pray. Amen.

The Truth About God

What a breath of fresh air it is to meet someone who is genuinely honest, real and truthful. God is such a Person, as the following Scriptures (and many, many others) attest:

He is the Rock, His work is perfect; for all His ways are justice, a God of truth and without injustice; righteous and upright is He (Deuteronomy 32:4, *NKJV*).

The sum of Your word is truth, and every one of Your righteous ordinances is everlasting (Psalm 119:160).

For the Law was given through Moses; grace and truth were realized through Jesus Christ (John 1:17).

And we know that the Son of God has come, and has given us understanding so that we may know Him who is true; and we are in Him who is true; in His Son Jesus Christ. This is the true God and eternal life (1 John 5:20).

Jesus described Himself in John 14:6 this way: "I am the way, and the *truth*, and the life" (emphasis added). That is either the most arrogant statement ever uttered on earth or the words of a madman—or the absolute truth. For Jesus did not merely say He was an honest man or that He spoke truth. He said He *is* the truth, and His resurrection backs up His claims about Himself. Jesus indeed is the truth; therefore, He is incapable of lying. When He opens His mouth, He speaks the truth, the whole truth and nothing but the truth. That means we can stake our lives on His Word. That's good news, because our lives do indeed depend on His Word.

The Truth About You

Many times we find ourselves looking at the Word of God and thinking, *I wish that could be true*, or *I just wish I could believe that*. When we have been through painful trials or traumatic times, our faith level may be quite low. We easily fall prey to doubt and become double-minded and unstable in all our ways (see James

1:6-8). In such a state, we see little if any evidence of answered prayer, so the enemy discourages us from even trying. We shut our Bibles with a sigh and wonder how it is that others can have such strong faith.

If this has been your struggle, I have great news for you! You do not have to allow your mind to be bullied by the devil's deadly duo of doubt and deception anymore. Why not? Consider what God's Word says about you:

> For God has not given us a spirit of fear, but of power and of love and of a sound mind (2 Timothy 1:7, *NKJV*).

> This is the covenant that I will make with them after those days, says the LORD: I will put My laws upon their heart, and upon their mind I will write them (Hebrews 10:16).

> But when He, the Spirit of truth, comes, He will guide you into all the truth; for He will not speak on His own initiative, but whatever He hears, He will speak; and He will disclose to you what is to come (John 16:13).

> But he who is spiritual appraises all things, yet he himself is appraised by no one. For who has known the mind of the LORD, that he will instruct Him? But we have the mind of Christ (1 Corinthians 2:15-16).

Let's sum up what these verses are saying. In Christ, God has given you a sound mind, and upon that mind He reveals His truth. When you live by the Spirit's power, He guides you into the truth and enables you to function with the very mind of Christ. He enables you to examine and understand things around you with clarity. You are able to walk by faith in the Father and His Word, because that is how Jesus lived, and you "have the mind of Christ" (1 Corinthians 2:16)!

The Truth About Freedom

Your mind is the main battleground where an intense war is being waged for control of your soul. Because you have the mind of Christ, you do not have to surrender your thought life to the devil. This is critical for you to realize. You are not a hopeless case. You are not doomed to be plagued by harassing, accusing, lustful or deceitful thoughts the rest of your life. There is freedom in Christ, and that freedom results in peace of mind.

A lazy, passive view of the Christian life will not cut it. God will not win this battle without our cooperation. We have to assume responsibility for our own thoughts, as per these biblical mandates:

- Make a continual practice of renewing your mind through the Word of God, for that is the way your life is transformed (see Romans 12:1-2).

- "[Take] every thought captive to the obedience of Christ," and examine it in the light of the Word of God under the guidance of the Spirit (2 Corinthians 10:5).

- Reject the lies and choose to dwell on the truth, because the truth will set you free (see Philippians 4:8; John 8:31-32).

Prayer for Today

Dear God, You are the truth through and through, and Your Word is absolutely true. I thank You that Your truth will set me free to be all that You created me to be. I refuse to believe the lie that my mind is incapable of knowing, understanding or believing Your truth. I have the mind of Christ, and I belong to You! Therefore, I choose to renew my mind according to Your Word, Lord, and I resist the devil's deceptions. I choose to wage war by putting on the belt of truth. Jesus, You are the truth, and Your Word is truth. I choose to abide in You; renew my mind with Your Word. And it's in the name of Jesus, who is the truth, that I pray. Amen.

DAILY SCRIPTURE READING:
ROMANS 2

Daily Journal

_____
_____
_____
_____
_____
_____
_____
_____
_____
_____
_____
_____
_____
_____
_____
_____
_____
_____
_____
_____
_____
_____

9

MORE POWER TO YA!

Our union with Jesus Christ is much more than positional truth. It is a living, daily reality! We have within us the very life of Christ. We have the awesome privilege of having fellowship with and drawing strength from the God who created the universe and who raised the Lord Jesus from the dead.

When we wait upon the Lord, we will renew our strength and "mount up with wings like eagles" (Isaiah 40:31). Let's take a moment to wait on Him in prayer right now:

Dear heavenly Father, You are my Lord and my God. You are the almighty Creator of heaven and earth. You spoke, and they were created; You speak now, and they remain. How awesome You are! Open my eyes today to the surpassing greatness of Your power toward all who believe in You. In the all-powerful name of Jesus my Lord, I pray. Amen.

The Truth About God

None of us will ever rise higher in our lives than our concept of God. What we believe to be true about Him is the most important part of our belief system. An anemic view of God will surely result in a weak and sickly faith. Let the words of the prophet Jeremiah energize you today as we focus on the mighty power of God!

> Ah, Sovereign LORD, you have made the heavens and the earth by your great power and outstretched arm. Nothing is too hard for you. You show love to thousands but bring the punishment for the fathers' sins into the laps of their children after them. O great and powerful God, whose name is the LORD Almighty, great are your purposes and mighty are your deeds (Jeremiah 32:17-19, *NIV*).

Notice the adjectives used to describe God: "sovereign," "great," "powerful," "almighty" and "mighty."

What are the issues that concern you today? Compared to creating the heavens and the earth, how great are your problems? Is God not able to handle anything that comes your way?

The apostle Paul prayed that we would know the awesome power of God. Notice the extent of this power that has been extended to all those who believe:

> I pray that the eyes of your heart may be enlightened, so that you will know what is the hope of His calling, what are the riches of the glory of His inheritance in the saints, and what is the surpassing greatness of His power toward us who believe. These are in accordance with the working of the strength of His might which He brought about in Christ, when He raised Him from the dead and seated Him at His right hand in the heavenly places, far above all rule and authority and power and dominion, and every name that is named, not only in this age but also in the one to come. And He put all things in subjection under His feet, and gave Him as head over all things to the church, which is His body, the fullness of Him who fills all in all (Ephesians 1:18-23).

Compared to raising Jesus from the dead and exalting Him with all authority in the universe to His right-hand throne, how great are your problems? Is He not more than able to handle them? Because of your position in Christ, are you not able to handle them?

The Truth About You

Often we picture the almighty God exercising power from His throne on high, and He does. But how often do we realize that His dynamic presence is at work within us? That is an astounding but absolutely true thought, as Ephesians 3:20-21 tells us:

> Now to Him who is able to do far more abundantly beyond all that we ask or think, according to the power that works within us, to Him be the glory in the church and in Christ Jesus to all generations forever and ever. Amen.

You may have developed habits of living by the flesh and believing the devil's lies. You may even see yourself as weak and prone to failure. But God wants you to break free from self-imposed limitations and realize that His mighty power is within you. Lay aside your self-sufficiency, and find your sufficiency in Christ as this verse teaches!

> But we have this treasure in earthen vessels [these fragile human bodies], so that the surpassing greatness of the power will be of God and not from ourselves (2 Corinthians 4:7).

If you are a born-again child of God, the Holy Spirit resides within you (see Romans 8:9). And the Holy Spirit is bearing witness with your spirit that you are a child of God (see Romans 8:16). So almighty God in all His power lives in you! Realizing that your soul is in union with God will make a difference in how you live.

The Truth About Freedom

"Now the Lord is the Spirit, and where the Spirit of the Lord is, there is liberty" (2 Corinthians 3:17). Many Christians don't realize that truth. Some view God as a cosmic killjoy who is determined to take all the fun out of their lives. It is true that God wants us to turn away from the passing pleasures of sin that lead to slavery, but that is so we can experience the real joy of true freedom. The more you realize that, the more you see that God's will is the path to the most satisfying, meaningful life possible.

The critical question is this: Though the Spirit of God is *resident* in your life, is He *Lord* of your life? Is He leading You into the truth that will set you free? Is He empowering you to live the Christian life, or are you relying on your own strength and resources?

You can choose to live according to the flesh, continuing to fall into the traps that the enemy cruelly sets, or you can walk by the Spirit and not carry out the desires of the flesh (see Galatians 5:16). Which is it going to be? The following Scripture verses make it clear that we are either living according to the Spirit or we are living according to the flesh, and there is no middle ground:

> For you were called to freedom, brethren; only do not turn your freedom into an opportunity for the flesh, but through love serve one another. . . . I say, walk by the Spirit, and you will not carry out the desire of the flesh. For the flesh sets its desire against the Spirit, and the Spirit against the flesh; for these are in opposition to one another, so that you may not do the things that you please (Galatians 5:13,16-17).

Are you tired of spiritual mediocrity? Are you ready for a change? The following prayer has no miracle-working powers, but God does! If you sincerely desire the fullness of the Spirit in your life, then praying this prayer in faith may be a significant moment for you. God bless you!

Prayer for Today

Dear heavenly Father, Your Son, the Lord Jesus, invited me to come to His presence when I am weary and heavy laden. When I try in my own strength to live the Christian life and meet all the demands and commands I see in Your Word, I feel crushed by the weight of responsibility. I feel discouraged by my inability to make any headway. I feel paralyzed by my own sinful desires that distract me time and time again.

Oh God, I cry out to You for the fullness of the Spirit! I long to have Your presence and power unleashed in and through me. Right now, Lord, I renounce seeking to live the Christian life in my own strength, and I choose to let You live in and through me. As the wind fills the sail of a boat to give it power and direction, I am pulling in the oars of self-effort, Lord, and hoisting the sail. Please cause the powerful wind of Your Spirit to blow in a fresh way within me. For Your glory and the furtherance of Your kingdom, I pray in Jesus' name. Amen.

DAILY SCRIPTURE READING:
ROMANS 3

Daily Journal

_____

_____

_____

_____

_____

_____

_____

Bitterness and unforgiveness are arguably the most prevalent freedom robbers in our Christian lives. We give the devil an opportunity in our lives when we let the sun go down on our anger, clinging tightly to our pain rather than releasing it to God (see Ephesians 4:26-27).

For a complete refresher course in what forgiveness is and is not, consult Step Three in the Steps to Freedom in Christ (see the back of this book). Here are some of the main points:

1. Forgiving someone does not mean we will necessarily forget what was done to us.

2. Forgiveness is a choice, a decision of the will, something that we can do because God commands us to do it.

3. Forgiveness means we let the other person off our hook, but they are not off God's hook.

4. Forgiveness is a matter of obedience to God, for our benefit, so we can be free from our past. We need to go ahead and make the choice to forgive, even if we don't feel like doing it.

5. Forgiving someone means that we agree to live with the (temporary) consequences of their sin. Christ already suffered the eternal consequences for their sin by His death on the cross.

6. Forgiveness must be exercised toward the offenders, even if they refuse (or are unable) to apologize.

7. Forgiving from the heart is necessary for freedom; it means we are honest about how the offense or offender made or makes us feel.

8. Forgiving others and showing them mercy should be our heart's response to having been forgiven and shown mercy by God for our offenses.

9. Forgiving ourselves may be crucial for our freedom; it means letting ourselves off the hook, accepting the truth that God has already forgiven us completely in Christ.

10. If there is anger in our hearts toward God, we need to let go of it, though we don't "forgive" God in the normal sense because He is perfect and sinless.

Will you commit yourself in prayer to allow God to bring to the surface any painful memories? Will you choose today to extend grace and forgiveness toward those who have hurt you?

Dear heavenly Father, I thank You for the riches of Your kindness, forbearance and patience toward me, knowing that Your kindness has led me to repentance. I confess that I have not shown that same kindness and patience toward those who have hurt me. Instead, I have held on to my anger, bitterness and resentment toward them. Please bring to my mind all the people I need to forgive so that I may do so now. In Jesus' name I pray. Amen.

For each person the Lord brings to your mind, including yourself, pray the following prayer out loud from your heart. Focus on each person on your forgiveness list until you cannot think of any other painful memories or offenses relating to them. Feel free to modify the prayer as needed when releasing anger held against God.

Dear Lord, I choose to forgive [name the person] for [say what the person did to hurt you], even though it made/makes me feel [describe the painful emotion]. I choose not to hold these things against [name the person] any longer. I thank You for setting me free from the bondage of my anger and bitterness toward [name]. I bless [name] now in Jesus' name. Amen.

1 0

THE HEART OF THE FATHER

Ever since the Garden of Eden, the devil has been working over-time to slander the reputation of God the Father in our eyes. He would delight in nothing more than for us to believe lies about the character of our heavenly Father, doubting His good-ness, power, love and faithfulness. For why would anyone want to come to an angry, cold, impatient or cruel God in prayer? So the enemy's assault on our concept of God is relentless.

Choose to start this day by confronting the lies we may have believed about our heavenly Father. Let's begin by praying that God would graciously move in our hearts:

Dear heavenly Father, I know that on this side of heaven, we will always see You as less than You are in all Your glorious majesty and holiness. But to the extent that it is possible to know You now as You really are, please reveal Yourself to me. I long to be free from these awful distortions of Your character that plague me with doubts, fears, worries and mistrust. Please expose every lie that I have believed about You, and set me free with Your truth so that I can worship You in spirit and in truth and come to You freely in prayer. In Jesus' name I pray. Amen.

The Truth About God

God is the Father you have always needed and wanted. The word "father," however, may or may not have pleasant memories attached to it for you. If it does, praise God! If it doesn't, God wants to reveal to you what He is really like so that you can learn to trust Him.

The following exercise is found in Step Three of the Steps to Freedom in Christ. It is placed there because very often we project onto God the character traits of the significant authorities in our lives. If those relationships have been hurtful or harmful, we may come to harbor anger toward God, believing He is just like those people. But once we do make the choice to forgive those who have hurt us, there is often a ripple effect that enables us to release our anger toward God and begin to genuinely believe the truths about our heavenly Father.

To help break down any walls that have been formed between you and God, read through the following lists out loud. Work your way down one by one, from left to right, prefacing the 11 phrases in the left column with "I renounce the lie that my Father God is" and prefacing the 11 phrases on the right with "I joyfully accept the truth that my Father God is."

We also encourage you to look up the Scripture references in parentheses.

I renounce the lie that my Father God is	I joyfully accept the truth that my Father God is
1. Distant and disinterested	1. Intimate and involved (Psalm 139:1-18)
2. Insensitive and uncaring	2. Kind and compassionate (Psalm 103:8-14)
3. Stern and demanding	3. Accepting and filled with joy and love (Zephaniah 3:17; Romans 15:7)
4. Passive and cold	4. Warm and affectionate (Isaiah 40:11; Hosea 11:3-4)
5. Absent or too busy for me	5. Always with me and eager to be with me (Jeremiah 31:20; Ezekiel 34:11-16; Hebrews 13:5)

I renounce the lie that my Father God is	I joyfully accept the truth that my Father God is
6. Never satisfied with what I do; impatient or angry	6. Patient and slow to anger (Exodus 34:6; 2 Peter 3:9)
7. Mean, cruel or abusive	7. Loving, gentle and protective of me (Psalm 18:2; Isaiah 42:3; Jeremiah 31:3)
8. Trying to take all the fun out of life	8. Trustworthy, wanting to give me a full life; His will is good, acceptable and perfect for me (Lamentations 3:22-23; John 10:10; Romans 12:1-2)
9. Controlling or manipulative	9. Full of grace and mercy, and He gives me freedom to fail (Luke 15:11-16; Hebrews 4:15-16)
10. Condemning or unforgiving	10. Tenderhearted, forgiving; His heart and arms are always open to me (Psalm 130:1-4; Luke 15:17-24)
11. Nitpicking, exacting or perfectionistic	11. Committed to my growth and proud of me as His growing child (Romans 8:28-29; 2 Corinthians 7:4; Hebrews 12:5-11)
I am the apple of His eye! (See Deuteronomy 32:9-10, *NIV*.)	

The Truth About You

In the Roman culture of Jesus' day, children were not treated with respect. Jesus, however, showed the Father's tender heart toward children when He held them, blessed them and warmly invited them to come to Him. So it should provide great encouragement to know that you are a child of God. May the following Scripture verses delight your heart today:

But as many as received Him, to them He gave the right to become children of God, even to those who believe in His name, who were born, not of blood nor of the will of the flesh nor of the will of man, but of God (John 1:12-13).

For you have not received a spirit of slavery leading to fear again, but you have received a spirit of adoption as sons by which we cry out, "Abba! Father!" (Romans 8:15).

For you are all sons of God through faith in Christ Jesus. For all of you who were baptized into Christ have clothed yourselves with Christ. There is neither Jew nor Greek, there is neither slave nor free man, there is neither male nor female; for you are all one in Christ Jesus. And if you belong to Christ, then you are Abraham's descendants, heirs according to promise (Galatians 3:26-29).

See how great a love the Father has bestowed on us, that we would be called children of God; and such we are. For this reason the world does not know us, because it did not know Him. Beloved, now we are children of God, and it has not appeared as yet what we will be. We know that when He appears, we will be like Him, because we will see Him just as He is (1 John 3:1-2).

Every believer in Jesus Christ is a child of the heavenly Father. We have been adopted into His family and cry out to Him, "Abba! Daddy! Father!"

We are also heirs of God and fellow heirs with Christ (see Romans 8:17). Obviously, we still are men or women of a certain nationality and occupation, but that is not our primary identity. At the core of our being, that is not who we are. We are children of God. So lift up your head, child of the King; you are a heavenly prince or princess! Though you may not feel as though you can measure up to the world's standards of what makes a valuable person, you are royalty in God's eyes! His eyes see clearly.

The Truth About Freedom

As we see the wonderful character of our heavenly Father and the incredible privilege we have of being His children, a whole new world opens up to us: the world of prayer. We are free to come confidently into the throne room and know that we are the beloved children of our Abba, Father.

As we approach the throne of our heavenly Father to receive merciful help in time of need, we find it is indeed a "throne of grace" (Hebrews 4:16). The blood of Jesus has opened wide the "prayer doors" for us (see Hebrews 10:19-22). The following Scripture verses about prayer show us how our God of mercy and grace is generously inviting us to pray:

> Ask, and it will be given to you; seek, and you will find; knock, and it will be opened to you. For everyone who asks receives, and he who seeks finds, and to him who knocks it will be opened. Or what man is there among you who, when his son shall ask him for a loaf, will give him a stone? Or if he asks for a fish, he will not give him a snake, will he? If you then, being evil, know how to give good gifts to your children, how much more will your Father who is in heaven give what is good to those who ask Him! (Matthew 7:7-11).

> Truly, truly, I say to you, he who believes in Me, the works that I do, he will do also; and greater works than these he will do; because I go to the Father. Whatever you ask in My name, that will I do, so that the Father may be glorified in the Son. If you ask Me anything in My name, I will do it (John 14:12-14).

You did not choose Me but I chose you, and appointed you that you would go and bear fruit, and that your fruit should remain, that whatever you ask of the Father in My name He may give to you (John 15:16).

Incredible promises! Jesus is saying that if we ask the Father for anything that Jesus would ask for, it is ours! What would happen if more of us really took God up on this offer?

Prayer for Today

Dear Father, that title "Father" now means more to me than ever. I thank You that through the shed blood of Your Son, I, too, am now Your child. I can call You my Father. And just as the Lord Jesus prayed to You and You heard Him, I know You will hear the prayers I pray in accordance with the character of Jesus.

Father, when I look at the vastness of Your prayer promises, I feel as though I'm trying to explore outer space with a kite. I am so tied down by my own small vision. Open my eyes, Lord, to the privilege I have of petitioning You in prayer. Set me free from my own unbelief so that I can pray in faith. In Jesus' name I truly pray. Amen.

DAILY SCRIPTURE READING:
ROMANS 4

Daily Journal

_____

_____

_____

_____

11

FROM NIGHT TO LIGHT

Walking with God is the privilege of every child of God! Enoch, the Old Testament saint, walked with God for 300 years (see Genesis 5:22). Incredible! If we truly want to walk with God, however, we must walk in the light, because God is light.

Let's begin today's lesson by committing ourselves to living in the light with God:

Dear heavenly Father, I want to walk with You today. Thank You that You love me enough not to sit back and let me stumble in the darkness. So I ask You today to search me, O God, and know my heart; try me and know my anxious thoughts. See if there be any hurtful way in me, and lead me in the everlasting way. Reveal to my mind the ways I am still walking in the darkness of pretense and hypocrisy. You know every intimate detail of my life and still love me passionately. I know that in Your light I will see the truth. In Jesus' name I pray. Amen.

The Truth About God

The letter of 1 John was written so that believers might know how to have close, intimate fellowship, or communion, with God and with one another. John starts out his letter by proclaiming what God is like:

This is the message we have heard from Him and announce to you, that God is Light, and in Him there is no darkness at all (1:5).

What does "God is Light" mean? Think of all that light does. It reveals the way things are. It dispels darkness. It enables us to see so that we can walk in freedom. It reveals the path ahead of us, cheers us up and dispels the fears of the unknown.

For the believer who is longing to walk with God, the light of God's presence brings great comfort, and His Word brings clear guidance:

The LORD is my light and my salvation; whom shall I fear? The LORD is the defense of my life; whom shall I dread? (Psalm 27:1).

Your word is a lamp to my feet and a light to my path (Psalm 119:105).

When we stray from the light and wander into the twilight or darkness, we find the brilliant searchlight of God's Word to be painfully blunt:

For the word of God is living and active and sharper than any two-edged sword, and piercing as far as the division of soul and spirit, of both joints and marrow, and able to judge the thoughts and intentions of the heart. And there is no creature hidden from His sight, but all things are open and laid bare to the eyes of Him with whom we have to do (Hebrews 4:12-13).

Initially, it may be painful when God exposes our deeds done in darkness, but the light of God's Word is always a liberating friend. In the darkness, we live in denial and shame, trying to justify ourselves and blaming others in order to defend ourselves; but Jesus shows us a better way to live—in the light with Him.

> Then Jesus again spoke to them, saying, "I am the Light of the world; he who follows Me will not walk in the darkness, but will have the Light of life" (John 8:12).

The Truth About You

How do you see yourself? Are you tempted to think of yourself as evil? Are you filled with a sense of shame and guilt? Do you believe that you are just a no-good, worthless, lousy sinner? The devil wants us to believe that nothing much has changed inside us, even though we are born-again. He tries to get us to believe the lie that we are evil and still belong to him. But nothing could be further from the truth, as the apostle Paul so clearly wrote:

> For you were formerly darkness, but now you are Light in the Lord; walk as children of Light (for the fruit of the Light consists in all goodness and righteousness and truth), trying to learn what is pleasing to the Lord (Ephesians 5:8-10).

The presence of God is the light of the world, and He has turned on the lights within you! Every believer in Christ is now a child of light. We no longer live in the domain of darkness but in the kingdom of God's beloved Son (see Colossians 1:13). We can no longer feel comfortable living in sin, deception and hypocrisy the way an unbeliever can, because it goes against our true nature as children of light.

Child of light, don't let the devil lure you back into the darkness. The devil's seductive whispers are lies. His demons are like roaches that disappear into the shadows when the light is turned on.

The Truth About Freedom

"God is Light and in Him there is no darkness at all" (1 John 1:5). To walk with God in freedom, we must also walk in the bright light of holiness and truth, where God walks. God will never compromise by taking one step into the darkness or even the twilight. We cannot have fellowship with Him if we live in secret sin, pretend we are something we are not or play the game of putting on a spiritual mask (hypocrisy). The path of freedom and fellowship with God and others is the path of truth, honesty, integrity, righteousness and authenticity. First John 1:6-9 puts it this way:

> If we say that we have fellowship with Him and yet walk in the darkness, we lie and do not practice the truth; but if we walk in the Light as He Himself is in the Light, we have fellowship with one another, and the blood of Jesus His Son cleanses us from all sin. If we say that we have no sin, we are deceiving ourselves and the truth is not in us. If we confess our sins, He is faithful and righteous to forgive us our sins and to cleanse us from all unrighteousness.

"Light living," as opposed to "darkness dwelling," is also the path to victorious spiritual warfare against sin, as Romans 13:12-14 teaches. We would do well to heed Paul's words:

> The night is almost gone, and the day is near. Therefore let us lay aside the deeds of darkness and put on the armor of light. Let us behave properly as in the day, not in carousing and drunkenness, not in sexual promiscuity and sensuality, not in strife and jealousy. But put on the Lord Jesus Christ, and make no provision for the flesh in regard to its lusts.

Prayer for Today

Dear heavenly Father, I thank You that You are light, and in You is absolutely no darkness. I here and now proclaim with great joy that I am Your child, a child of the light. You have delivered me from the domain of darkness and brought me into the kingdom of Jesus, the light of the world. I renounce all the unfruitful deeds of darkness and the things hidden because of shame. More than anything else, I want to have true, honest, open, real fellowship with You and my brothers and sisters in Christ. Thank You that as I walk in the light, I will have that fellowship; and the blood of Jesus, Your Son, will cleanse me from all sin. I choose today to let my light shine before men in such a way that they see my good works and glorify You, my Father in heaven. And it's in Jesus' name I pray. Amen.

DAILY SCRIPTURE READING:

ROMANS 5

Daily Journal

_____

_____

_____

_____

_____

_____

_____

_____

_____

_____

12

DIVINE LIVING

Jesus was the Master Teacher. He saw spiritual truth in the everyday world in which His disciples lived, and used those earthly things to teach heavenly realities. As you read through the Gospels, you see Him talking about doors, salt, sheep, houses, storms, lamps, grain, birds, flowers and many other common items.

Jesus used similes such as "The kingdom of heaven is like a mustard seed" (Matthew 13:31) and metaphors such as "I am the bread of life" (John 6:35) in order to hold the attention of His listeners and teach spiritual principles. Today, we are going to look at one of those metaphors of Jesus and seek to understand its deep ramifications for our lives as believers in Him. Let's pray toward that end:

Dear heavenly Father, I thank You that You are the Master Teacher who wants to guide me by Your Holy Spirit into all truth today. I ask You to open my eyes that I might behold the liberating truth of Your Word. May Your truth liberate me in areas where I do not even realize I need it. And I thank You for what You'll do. In Jesus' name I pray. Amen.

The Truth About God

Grapes, wine and vineyards played an integral part in the life of a first-century Jew in Israel. So when Jesus spoke the following words in John 15, His followers could relate:

I am the true vine, and My Father is the vinedresser (v. 1).

I am the vine, you are the branches; he who abides in Me
and I in him, he bears much fruit, for apart from Me you
can do nothing (v. 5).

Jesus identifies Himself as "the vine," even "the true vine."
Such imagery enabled His disciples to learn something very important about their relationship with Him.

The vine is what connects the roots with the branches. The
roots are that which extract the life-giving nutrients from the
soil so that the branches can bear fruit. The vine or trunk of
any plant or tree supports the whole so that it can grow strong
and tall, reaching up toward the light of the sun. It also provides the conduit through which nutrients flow from the soil
to the branch. A branch has no hope of bearing fruit if it is cut
off from the vine.

Jesus wants us to know where the support, strength and sus-
tenance of life come from—from Him and Him alone! He alone
can provide what we need to bear spiritual fruit. Just as the sap
flows from the vine to the branches, enabling it to bear fruit, so
life flows from Jesus into us.

What is the vinedresser's role? He makes sure the soil in
which the vines are planted is good soil. He makes sure there is
ample sun and water. He pulls out weeds that would be destructive to the plant. He prunes back the unproductive branches
so that the grapevine will bear even more fruit. In the end, he
stands back and observes with great joy the rich harvest the
plant produces.

God our Father is our Gardener-Provider. He takes care of
the whole body of believers, giving special attention to each one
individually. He strengthens us and protects us from the evil
one. He tills the soil of our hearts so that we are open and re-
ceptive to the light and water of the Word. He disciplines us in

love so that we will bear even more good fruit. He also expresses great joy and is glorified when His children bear fruit.

The Truth About You

We have looked at verses 1 and 5 of John 15. Now let's see what is sandwiched in between:

> Every branch in Me that does not bear fruit, He takes away; and every branch that bears fruit, He prunes it so that it may bear more fruit. You are already clean because of the word which I have spoken to you. Abide in Me, and I in you. As the branch cannot bear fruit of itself unless it abides in the vine, so neither can you unless you abide in Me (vv. 2-4).

One of the great themes of the New Testament is that true believers in Jesus are "in Christ." Jesus is using the relationship of the vine and branches to teach and illustrate that truth. If you take a look at a grapevine, you will see that it is hard to determine exactly where the vine ends and the branch begins. Essentially, they are one. The branches grow out of all different parts of the vine and end up being interwoven with each other.

What a wonderful picture of our relationship with Jesus and with one another! We are in Christ, He is in us, and we are in each other! We are already clean, Jesus says, because of the word He spoke to us—the word of salvation. Praise the Lord!

The Truth About Freedom

Freedom in Christ results in bearing much fruit. The same truth is taught in Romans 7:4:

> Therefore, my brethren, you also were made to die to the Law through the body of Christ, so that you might

be joined to another, to Him who was raised from the dead, in order that we might bear fruit for God.

No real fruit is born in our lives when we live in bondage to sin, live according to our flesh, or live under the Law. We bear fruit only when we abide in Jesus!

What does "abide in Christ" mean? It means to stay connected to, remain with, depend on and draw strength from Jesus. It is living our daily lives in the reality of being in union with Him. The primary mark of the abiding Christian is a life free to love God and other people. Jesus expressed this clearly in John 15:9-12:

Just as the Father has loved Me, I have also loved you; abide in My love. If you keep My commandments, you will abide in My love; just as I have kept My Father's commandments and abide in His love. These things I have spoken to you so that My joy may be in you, and that your joy may be made full. This is My commandment, that you love one another, just as I have loved you.

Do you want to experience the love of God on a moment-by-moment basis, just as Jesus did? Then live a life of obedience, just as Jesus did! Trusting and obeying God results in loving others. In this way, we show that we truly love God. How does this affect us personally? The joy of Jesus will be in us, and that joy will be full!

Where can you find strength to live such a life? From abiding in Jesus, the Vine. He is the source of life and strength. You are already in Him. Will you abide in Him?

Prayer for Today

Loving heavenly Father, I thank You that You are so committed to my care and growth. I want to abide in You and in Your Son, the Lord Jesus. Where else could I go? You have words of eternal life. I joyfully accept my place as a branch connected to Jesus, the Vine. I long to bear much fruit that would remain, and in so doing bring glory and honor to You. Knowing I cannot bear fruit of myself, I choose today to trust and rely on Jesus and to obey His command to love others in the power of the Holy Spirit. I see from Your Word that this is the path to experiencing the full joy of Jesus, the true Vine. And it's in His name I pray. Amen.

DAILY SCRIPTURE READING:
ROMANS 6

Daily Journal

_____
_____
_____
_____
_____
_____
_____
_____
_____
_____
_____
_____
_____
_____
_____
_____
_____
_____
_____

FREEDOM
REFRESHER
={FOUR}=

In our society, television commercials and movies sometimes extol the "virtues" of the independent hero who goes his own way and makes his own laws. In many ways, such a character lives out the secret fantasy of many Americans. However, what may seem admirable and thrilling to the flesh may be deadly to a life of freedom in Christ.

Scripture clearly teaches that all authority has been established by God. So what should our responsibility be? Romans 13:1 says, "Every person is to be in subjection to the governing authorities." First Peter 2:16-17 teaches that our freedom in Christ does not grant us the license to do as we please, contrary to what some people believe:

> Act as free men, and do not use your freedom as a covering for evil, but use it as bondslaves of God. Honor all people, love the brotherhood, fear God, honor the king.

Our submission to authority must be "not with external service, as those who merely please men, but with sincerity of heart, fearing the Lord" (Colossians 3:22).

To reaffirm your commitment to walk in submission to the authorities God has placed in your life, will you pray the following prayer?

> *Dear heavenly Father, You have said in Your Word that rebellion is the same thing as witchcraft and as bad as idolatry. I know that I have not always obeyed You in this area, and I have rebelled in attitude and in action against You and against those You have placed in authority over me.*

Thank You for Your forgiveness of my rebellion. By the shed blood of the Lord Jesus Christ, I pray that all ground gained by evil spirits in my life due to my rebellion would be ceded back to You. I pray that You would show me specifically any and all ways that I have been rebellious. I choose now to adopt a submissive spirit and a servant's heart. In Jesus' name I pray. Amen.

Is the Lord showing you that you have had a rebellious attitude toward the government, its leaders or its laws? Wives, what has your attitude been toward your husband and his authority? Husbands, have you fostered an unresponsive, cold or non-submissive heart to the needs of your wife through a lack of love and tenderness?

Have you harbored a rebellious heart that stubbornly refuses to submit to your boss, teacher or coach? What has your attitude been toward your parents, stepparents or legal guardians? Have you been in rebellion against church leadership in any way?

Finally, have you been a hearer and not a doer of the Word? Are you submissive to the will of God in your life?

For any and all areas of rebellion the Lord brings to your mind, pray the following prayer out loud from your heart:

Dear Lord, I confess that I have been rebellious toward [name the specific person(s) against whom you have rebelled] by [be specific in stating what you did or the attitude you had]. Thank You for forgiving my rebellion. I choose now to be submissive to all governing authorities and to Your Word with all my heart. In Jesus' name I pray. Amen.

13

STAND FIRM AND FIGHT!

Some of the paintings of Jesus portray a man with stringy hair, pale skin, a frail-looking body and sad eyes. Not the kind of Jesus that moves you to worship and respect. He looks more like a man in need than a man we need!

All of us at times entertain images in our minds that cause us to see Jesus as less than He really is. We may picture Him as meek, mild, calm, passionless and harmless. In our more honest moments, we may wonder if Jesus is tough enough to take on the devil and win the spiritual battles of life. Well, be encouraged—the Lord Jesus is indeed a victorious warrior! Let's ask God to open our minds to this aspect of His character:

Dear heavenly Father, I am fighting fierce, daily battles in my mind. I am seeking to walk with You, but the enemy seems to oppose me at every turn. I need a fresh vision of You that will give me the strength to live victoriously in Christ. I want to see You in Your armor and watch the enemy tremble before You. I look forward to what You'll teach me today. In Jesus' name I pray. Amen.

The Truth About God

The Hebrew people had just escaped from the bondage of Egypt, but now they were confronted with an "impossible" dilemma. In front of them was the impassable Red Sea; to their rear, the furiously approaching Egyptian army. Then God stepped in, and the rest is His story. After the Hebrew people crossed over on dry land and watched the drowned army wash up on shore, spontaneous praise sprang forth from the hearts of God's people:

> I will sing to the LORD, for he is highly exalted. The horse and its rider he has hurled into the sea. The LORD is my strength and my song; he has become my salvation. He is my God, and I will praise him, my father's God, and I will exalt him. The LORD is a warrior; the LORD is his name. . . . Your right hand, O LORD, was majestic in power. Your right hand, O LORD, shattered the enemy. In the greatness of your majesty you threw down those who opposed you (Exodus 15:1-3,6,7, *NIV*).

You may be thinking, *Okay, that's the Old Testament. What about the New Testament? What about Jesus? How well can He handle Himself when confronted by the enemy?* The devil surely shudders when he thinks of the day when the Lord Jesus will come in judgment:

> And I saw heaven opened, and behold, a white horse, and He who sat on it is called Faithful and True, and in righteousness He judges and wages war. His eyes are a flame of fire, and on His head are many diadems; and He has a name written upon Him which no one knows except Himself. He is clothed with a robe dipped in blood, and His name is called The Word of God. And the armies which are in heaven, clothed in fine linen, white and clean, were following Him on white horses. From His mouth comes a sharp sword, so that with it He may strike down the nations, and He will rule them with a rod of iron; and He treads the wine press of the fierce wrath of God, the Almighty. And on His robe and

on His thigh He has a name written, "KING OF KINGS, AND LORD OF LORDS" (Revelation 19:11-16).

Convinced yet? The Lord Jesus, who came to destroy the devil's works, will come again at the final judgment. All His enemies will be thrown into the lake of fire forever, and Jesus will have triumphed. For now, we can rejoice that our names are written in the Lamb's book of life and that Satan is a defeated foe, stripped of his weapons by Jesus at the cross:

And having disarmed the powers and authorities, he made a public spectacle of them, triumphing over them by the cross (Colossians 2:15, *NIV*).

The Truth About You

Christ's victory over sin, death and Satan is ultimately ours as well. In this world, we will struggle with and at times even give in to sin. Unless Jesus returns first, we will all physically die. The devil may succeed in tempting, accusing or deceiving us. But in the end, the victory is ours. Meditate long on these truths, and rejoice in hope:

Who shall separate us from the love of Christ? Shall trouble or hardship or persecution or famine or nakedness or danger or sword? As it is written: "For your sake we face death all day long; we are considered as sheep to be slaughtered." No, in all these things we are more than conquerors through him who loved us. For I am convinced that neither death nor life, neither angels nor demons, neither the present nor the future, nor any powers, neither height nor depth, nor anything else in all creation, will be able to separate us from the love of God that is in Christ Jesus our Lord (Romans 8:35-39, *NIV*).

When this happens, then at last this Scripture will come true—"Death is swallowed up in victory." O death, where then your victory? Where then your sting? For sin—the sting that causes death—will all be gone; and the law, which reveals our sins, will no longer be our judge. How we thank God for all of this! It is he who makes us victorious through Jesus Christ our Lord! (1 Corinthians 15:54-57, *TLB*).

Through our faith in Jesus, we have overcome the world (see 1 John 5:4), crucified the flesh with its passions and desires (see Galatians 5:24), and stand in the One who rendered "powerless him who had the power of death, that is, the devil" (Hebrews 2:14). Praise His glorious name!

The Truth About Freedom

Though Christ has won the war and the outcome is sure, Satan still holds territory on planet Earth. His efforts to gain control over what he has lost (the souls of the saints) are relentless. He controls through deception. We sin when we believe his lies. If we don't confess and repent of our sins, we give back to the powers of darkness ground on which to operate. We stop that process by renouncing his lies and obeying James 4:7, which says, "Submit therefore to God. Resist the devil and he will flee from you."

We submit to God by abiding in Jesus, walking with Him in the power of the Spirit and the truth of His Word. We quickly confess and repent of sin and renounce all efforts to live the Christian life in our own strength and for our own glory. Then we can resist the devil, and he must flee from us! Yet how do we resist the devil? We resist when we put on the full armor of God:

Finally, be strong in the Lord and in the strength of His might. Put on the full armor of God, so that you will be able to stand firm against the schemes of the devil. For our struggle is not against flesh and blood, but against the rulers, against the powers, against the world forces of this darkness, against the spiritual forces of wickedness in the heavenly places. Therefore, take up the full armor of God, so that you will be able to resist in the evil day, and having done everything, to stand firm. Stand firm therefore, having girded your loins with truth, and having put on the breastplate of righteousness, and having shod your feet with the preparation of the gospel of peace; in addition to all, taking up the shield of faith with which you will be able to extinguish all the flaming arrows of the evil one. And take the helmet of salvation, and the sword of the Spirit, which is the word of God (Ephesians 6:10-17).

The battle cry for freedom has been sounded. Put on God's full armor. Stand firm! Resist! All the power of God is behind you, and Christ has already defeated the devil at the cross. The armor of God is invincible, and you can begin putting it on right now in prayer.

Prayer for Today

Dear Father, my victorious Lord and King, I praise You that You have won the war against evil and the evil one through Your Son's death, resurrection and ascension to the throne. I thank You that You have given me Your invincible armor to wear. I choose to put on the belt of truth, filling my mind with Your Word. I choose the path of righteousness and recognize that in Christ I am the righteousness of God. I put on the sandals of peace, knowing I have peace with You through Jesus. I reject all anxious thoughts, and I choose to thank and trust You to fill me with peace.

I keep the shield of faith ready to be taken up when the attacks come. Thank You that no fiery dart of the devil can penetrate it. I take up the helmet of salvation and claim Your protection over my mind. I will use the sword of the Spirit, the spoken Word of God, against all the devil's lies.

I stand alert and watchful in prayer, for myself as well as for my brothers and sisters in Christ. I will be strong in You and in Your mighty resurrection power through the Holy Spirit who lives in me. In Jesus' name I pray. Amen.

DAILY SCRIPTURE READING:
ROMANS 7

Daily Journal

14

THE MAJESTY AND
THE GLORY

The most significant characteristic of God is His holiness. The desire of Satan is to rob God of His glory. Once the angel Lucifer had great glory in heaven (see Ezekiel 28:12-14), but he wasn't satisfied with that. He wanted the glory of God Himself (see Isaiah 14:12-14), something neither he nor anyone else can ever have. So he was cast down from his lofty position, and he has furiously resented that indignity ever since.

The true angels of God still proclaim, however: "Holy, Holy, Holy, is the LORD of hosts, the whole earth is full of His glory" (Isaiah 6:3). We, as God's children, need to see our glorious and majestic God as He truly is; and that is the theme of today's opening prayer:

Dear heavenly Father, who is like You among the gods, O Lord? Who is like You, majestic in holiness, awesome in praises, working wonders? You are great and glorious, and Your glory indeed fills the earth. As Your child, I long to see Your glory and glorify Your holy name. I eagerly look to Your Word and ask You to show me Your glory. In Jesus' name I pray. Amen.

The Truth About God

In a once-in-a-lifetime moment of intimacy between God and man, the Lord revealed Himself to His servant Moses. Let's look in on this rare event of revelation:

> And the LORD said to Moses, "I will do the very thing
> you have asked [for God's Presence to go with them], be-
> cause I am pleased with you and I know you by name."
> Then Moses said, "Now show me your glory." And the
> LORD said, "I will cause all my goodness to pass in front
> of you, and I will proclaim my name, the Lord, in your
> presence" (Exodus 33:17-19, *NIV*).

The glory of God is a manifestation of His presence, which
reveals His goodness. It is captured in His name, the Lord, the
eternal, self-existent One, who covenants with His chosen to be
their Savior and Father.

You might be tempted to think that His glory is nice but
not overwhelming, but let's continue reading:

> "But," [God] said, "you cannot see my face, for no one
> may see me and live." Then the LORD said, "There is a
> place near me where you may stand on a rock. When
> my glory passes by, I will put you in a cleft in the rock
> and cover you with my hand until I have passed by.
> Then I will remove my hand and you will see my back;
> but my face must not be seen" (vv. 20-23, *NIV*).

Then the marvelous moment came when the glory of the
Lord descended in a cloud and passed by Moses, declaring:

> The LORD, the LORD, the compassionate and gracious
> God, slow to anger, abounding in love and faithfulness,
> maintaining love to thousands, and forgiving wicked-
> ness, rebellion and sin. Yet he does not leave the guilty
> unpunished (34:6-7, *NIV*).

What was Moses' response to this glorious revelation? He bowed down at once to the ground and worshiped (see v. 8). We would do the same if we beheld His glory, for God is worthy of all praise and honor and glory and worship. He is the majestic and glorious Lord who says, "I am the Lord, that is My name; I will not give My glory to another, nor My praise to graven images" (Isaiah 42:8).

The Truth About You

What were we created and redeemed to do? The *Westminster Shorter Catechism* teaches that the chief end (purpose) of man is to "glorify God and enjoy Him forever." God Himself proclaimed this truth in Isaiah 43:5-7:

> Do not fear, for I am with you; I will bring your offspring from the east, and gather you from the west. I will say to the north, "Give them up!" And to the south, "Do not hold them back." Bring My sons from afar and My daughters from the ends of the earth, everyone who is called by My name, and whom I have created for My glory, whom I have formed, even whom I have made.

What a high calling! God is summoning His children from the ends of the earth, bringing them to Himself, that He might be glorified.

Child of God, don't accept any lower calling on your life. Having been raised to sit with Christ on His throne, don't stoop to "walk in the counsel of the wicked, nor stand in the path of sinners, nor sit in the seat of scoffers!" (Psalm 1:1). Having been given the great privilege of glorifying the King of kings and Lord of lords, don't bow down to the gods of popularity, possessions, position, power or prestige. It is beneath you, child of the King!

The Truth About Freedom

If we were created for God's glory (and we were) and if we were saved and adopted into His family to the praise of the glory of His grace (and we were), what would God want to set us free to do? To glorify Him, of course!

We glorify God by manifesting His presence in our lives and by pointing people to the greatness and goodness of God by the way we live. For example, sexual immorality never glorifies God, but sexual fidelity and enjoyment in marriage do (see 1 Corinthians 6:15-20). That is just one instance of how our bodies can be used either for righteousness or unrighteousness. How we relate to food is another area of concern, as Paul discusses in his first letter to the Corinthians: "Whether, then, you eat or drink or whatever you do, do all to the glory of God" (10:31).

How do we do that? The apostle shines light on this very question: "All things are lawful for me, but not all things are profitable. All things are lawful for me, but I will not be mastered by anything" (6:12).

In Christ we have great freedom to enjoy life and the good gifts God has given to us. In their proper place, enjoyment of food, sex, hobbies, exercise, friendships, work, family, houses and so on is God's desire for us. He is glorified when we enjoy His good and perfect gifts (see James 1:17).

We run into serious problems, however, when we end up enjoying the gift more than the Giver. This is idolatry, or giving "praise to graven images" (Isaiah 42:8). The warning about this in Deuteronomy 8:7-20 ought to be read and reread by every Christian, particularly those of us who live in the United States.

Ask the Lord to shine His light on these areas of His gifts to you. Are you engaging in any behavior that is unprofitable? Are you mastered by anything? Remember: If you can't give up something, you don't own it—it owns you.

Prayer for Today

(Based in Part on Psalm 29)

Most glorious and majestic Lord, I bow before You and worship You. I realize that I was formed for Your glory and not my own. I choose therefore to glorify You in my body. Set me free from anything and everything that is more important to me than You so that I may not give my praise to graven images. As an expression of my sincere desire to glorify You, I choose to praise You for who You really are.

I ascribe to You, Lord, glory and strength. I ascribe to You the glory due Your name. I worship You in the splendor of Your holiness. Your voice, O Lord, is upon the waters. You, God of glory, thunder! Your voice is powerful and majestic. You shake the trees, and Your voice sends out flames of fire. Your powerful voice strips the leaves from the trees. And everything in Your temple cries out, "Glory!"

In the name of Him whose name is above every name, Jesus Christ, I pray. Amen.

DAILY SCRIPTURE READING:

ROMANS 8

Daily Journal

_____

_____

_____

_____

_____

_____

_____

THE GOD OF ALL WISDOM

Does God really know what He is doing? That sounds like a silly question since God is omniscient (all-knowing). However, the question takes on a personal meaning when things aren't going the way we had hoped or planned.

God has a way of shaking up our world when we become self-righteous or secure in our own strength and resources. When you find yourself dozing off in the lazy, warm sunshine, you may hear the rumble of distant thunder. Then when the storms of life hit, we wonder, *Does God really know what He is doing?* You may be struggling with that issue right now. Or if you are not, one day you very likely will. We can always be completely honest with God. Let's do so now in prayer:

Dear heavenly Father, I must admit there are times when I can't understand why You do what You do. There are aspects of my body and personality I don't like and wish were different. There are things in my past that are too painful to think about. There are times when things happen in my life that leave me confused and frustrated. Where is Your wisdom in all this? Please give me understanding so I can rest in You. In Jesus' name I pray. Amen.

The Truth About God

The dictionary defines wisdom as the "power of judging rightly and following the soundest course of action, based on knowledge, experience and understanding." Surely that is what we need in times of trouble. The apostle Paul, at the conclusion of writing about the future salvation of Israel, exploded with praise to God:

> Oh, the depth of the riches of the wisdom and knowl-edge of God! How unsearchable his judgments, and his paths beyond tracing out! "Who has known the mind of the Lord? Or who has been his counselor?" (Romans 11:33-34, *NIV*).

Isaiah echoed the same sentiment when he quoted God's de-scription of Himself:

> "For my thoughts are not your thoughts, neither are your ways my ways," declares the LORD. "As the heavens are higher than the earth, so are my ways higher than your ways and my thoughts than your thoughts" (Isaiah 55:8-9, *NIV*).

As we grow in our Christian lives, we all come face to face with the reality that God's ways are *different* from man's ways. It is only by faith that we come to rest in the reality that His ways are *higher* and *better* than our ways.

Colossians 2:3 says that "all the treasures of wisdom and knowledge" are hidden in Christ. Who can deny the incredible wisdom of God in sending His Son to die on the cross to res-cue fallen humanity from the chains of sin and death? Who could have thought of such a plan? Only God! Truly, even when God seems to be acting foolishly, His plans are far wiser than the greatest wisdom of men or angels (see 1 Corinthians 1:25; 2:7-8).

Many times we have things all figured out—or so we think—and then God changes the course of our lives. We fuss and fume and even get angry with God sometimes because He refuses to put His stamp of approval on our plans. But when the dust settles and the smoke clears, we can look back and see how He works all things together for our good (see Romans 8:28). We shake our heads in amazement at the awesome genius of His ways and His timing. He indeed is the God of all wisdom!

The Truth About You

Do you feel good about yourself? I mean, *really*. If you had three wishes and could change anything about your appearance or talents or giftedness, for what would you wish? Do you find yourself comparing yourself to others? Do you secretly wish you could be like them? Do you struggle with the sin of envy? We have all struggled with envy at times. For some of us, it may be a real controlling issue. Have you ever felt like Scar in the movie *The Lion King*, who said he felt as if he had come out of the "shallow end of the gene pool"?

We need to remove the blinders from our eyes so that we can see ourselves as the God of wisdom sees us:

I will give thanks to You, for I am fearfully and wonderfully made; wonderful are Your works, and my soul knows it very well (Psalm 139:14).

Shall the potter be considered as equal with the clay, that what is made should say to its maker, "He did not make me"; or what is formed say to him who formed it, "He has no understanding"? (Isaiah 29:16).

"Can I not, O house of Israel, deal with you as this potter does?" declares the LORD. "Behold, like the clay in the potter's hand, so are you in My hand, O house of Israel" (Jeremiah 18:6).

For we are His workmanship, created in Christ Jesus for good works, which God prepared beforehand so that we should walk in them (Ephesians 2:10).

Like clay in the hands of a master potter, so are we in the hands of God. We are God's masterpieces, His workmanship, His poems (from the Greek word *poiema*, in Ephesians 2:10). Each and every one of us was created to express the wisdom of God and glorify Him in our bodies. Indeed we are fearfully and wonderfully made.

The Truth About Freedom

Accepting yourself is a critical key to freedom. Take a minute to reflect on your physical body, personality, experiences or abilities (or inabilities!) that you have disliked or resented. We are not talking about the sinful flesh patterns we have created; we are talking about the aspects of God's unique creation in you.

Now offer each one to God, thanking Him for His wisdom in creating you the way He did, and asking Him to use that aspect of yourself for His glory. To say "thank You" to God for the parts of your body or personality that you would change if you could is an expression of faith. Doing so can be a very healing moment for you.

Prayer for Today

Dear heavenly Father, You are the Potter and I am the clay. Please forgive me for doubting Your wisdom in making me or for resenting Your sculpting of my life. I thank You that I am fearfully and wonderfully made and that all things indeed are working for good in my life. Your ways and thoughts are much higher than mine, so I choose to rest in You and Your ways. You indeed are at work in me both to will and to work for Your good pleasure. Do what You will in me, Lord, for Your glory. In Jesus' name I pray. Amen.

DAILY SCRIPTURE READING:

ROMANS 9

Daily Journal

_____
_____
_____
_____
_____
_____
_____
_____
_____
_____
_____
_____
_____
_____
_____
_____
_____
_____
_____
_____
_____
_____
_____
_____
_____
_____
_____

Fleshly pride is the one thing that is most contrary to Jesus Christ and the Christian life. Jesus described Himself as being "gentle and humble in heart" (Matthew 11:29). The prophet Micah declared that there was no secret to living the life that pleases God when he wrote, "He has told you, O man, what is good; and what does the LORD require of you but to do justice, to love kindness, and to walk humbly with your God?" (Micah 6:8).

God spoke through the prophet Isaiah, proclaiming that humility is what makes us noticeable to Him:

> But to this one I will look, to him who is humble and contrite of spirit, and who trembles at My word (Isaiah 66:2).

God is, in fact, opposed to the proud and self-sufficient person, but He gives grace to those who are humble (see James 4:6; 1 Peter 5:5). What is humility? Humility is the state of sincere dependence upon God rather than on self. It results in deeds of gentleness and kindness to others. Living a life of humility is absolutely essential to walking with God in the fullness of the Holy Spirit. If it is your genuine desire to humble yourself before God, then we invite you to pray:

Dear heavenly Father, Your Word declares that pride goes before destruction and an arrogant spirit before stumbling. I confess that many times I have thought mainly of myself and not of others. I have tried to live my life leaning on my own understanding rather than trusting You with all my heart. Too often, I have been self-centered and self-reliant rather than other-centered and dependent upon You.

I repent of my pride and self-sufficiency, and I pray that all ground gained in my members by the enemies of the Lord Jesus would be ceded back to me. I choose to rely on the Spirit's power and guidance so that I will do nothing from selfishness or empty conceit, but with humility of mind, I will regard others as more important than myself. And I choose to make You, Lord, the most important One in all my life.

What are the ways, Father, in which I am sinning in the area of pride? Please show me now that I might be like Jesus, who is gentle and humble in heart. And it's in His name I pray. Amen.

Quietly let the Lord search your heart. Think about how you live at home, at work, at school, at church, and so on. In what ways do you look down on others or react with a harsh, critical or belittling spirit? Are you stubborn and unteachable? Are you selfish with your time, money, possessions or affection? Do you boast of your accomplishments to draw attention to yourself? Are you easily wounded when you do not receive the attention, praise or glory you think you deserve? Self-pity is a form of pride. Do you cling to the "right" to be right, or do you dominate conversations with topics you know well? Are you a controlling person, trying to manipulate others into doing what you want them to do?

For anything and everything the Lord brings to mind, pray the following prayer out loud:

Dear Lord, I agree that I have been proud and self-serving in [name the specific ways]. Thank You for forgiving me for my pride. I choose to humble myself before You and others. I choose to place all my confidence in You and none in my flesh. In Jesus' humble name I pray. Amen.

SAFE AND SECURE

Nine out of 10 Americans believe that the world is a less safe place to live in now than when they were growing up. Almost half feel unsafe taking a walk alone at night within a half mile of their home. Although the reasons people feel afraid vary somewhat—based on current news stories—fears of being in a car crash, having cancer, inadequate Social Security, not having enough money for retirement and being a victim of violence consistently rank high.

What is God's plan to protect us, as things seem to be going from bad to worse? What should be our reaction to the increasing dangers of life? We need to pray and ask for God's peace and wisdom:

Dear heavenly Father, thank You that You are on Your throne. You are my ever-present help in times of danger, and because of You I have nothing to fear. You are my Father and You are my Shepherd, and You are completely willing and totally able to protect me. Enable me to see and believe these truths in a new and fresh way today so that I can be filled with Your peace and not be controlled by fear. In the name of Jesus, the Prince of Peace, I pray. Amen.

The Truth About God

There is perhaps no more comforting name for God than "Shepherd." Realizing the significance of that name can bring a sense of peace and serenity to our souls. The creator God and Lord of the universe is our personal Shepherd. Comfort yourself a little today by doing a bit of scriptural soul soothing as you gaze upon the Shepherd and Guardian of your soul (see 1 Peter 2:25).

> Like a shepherd He will tend His flock, in His arm He will gather the lambs and carry them in His bosom; He will gently lead the nursing ewes (Isaiah 40:11).

> The LORD is my shepherd, I shall not be in want. He makes me lie down in green pastures, he leads me beside quiet waters, he restores my soul. He guides me in paths of righteousness for his name's sake. Even though I walk through the valley of the shadow of death, I will fear no evil, for you are with me; your rod and your staff, they comfort me (Psalm 23:1-4, *NIV*).

The things the shepherd does for the flock, our God does for us. He takes care of us, making sure we have our physical needs met. But He does much more. He takes us to places of rest so that our souls as well as our bodies are refreshed, restored and renewed. He takes us down the right roads of wise guidance. Even when we are in danger, there is no need to fear, because He will never leave us nor forsake us (see Hebrews 13:5). He wards off our enemies with His rod and rescues us from the traps of life with His staff. When we are weak or frail or needy, He picks us up and carries us through those times with His peaceful presence.

The most remarkable thing about the Good Shepherd, the Lord Jesus Christ, is that He became like one of us sheep. He laid down His life for the sheep (see John 10:15) and thus became the Lamb of God, slaughtered for our sins.

> Worthy is our "God of peace, who brought up from the dead the great Shepherd of the sheep through the

blood of the eternal covenant, even Jesus our Lord" (Hebrews 13:20).

Worthy is the Lamb that was slain (Revelation 5:12).

For the Lamb in the center of the throne will be their shepherd, and will guide them to springs of the water of life; and God will wipe every tear from their eyes (Revelation 7:17).

The Truth About You

The Bible calls us sheep. Not the most flattering thing in the world, to be sure, but true nonetheless. You see, sheep easily stray away from safety and wander into danger. So do we. In addition, sheep are about as vulnerable a creature as exists. We are, too. Those are just two of the many good reasons why sheep need a shepherd—and why we need Jesus!

Sheep, however, do have one very endearing, lifesaving quality: Once they learn the shepherd's voice, they refuse to follow anyone else. Jesus referred to that particular trait of sheep when He spoke of our relationship to Him:

But he who enters by the door is a shepherd of the sheep. To him the doorkeeper opens, and the sheep hear his voice, and he calls his own sheep by name and leads them out. When he puts forth all his own, he goes ahead of them, and the sheep follow him because they know his voice. A stranger they simply will not follow, but will flee from him, because they do not know the voice of strangers. My sheep hear My voice, and I know them, and they follow Me; and I give eternal life to them, and they will never perish; and no one will snatch them out of My hand (John 10:2-5,27-28).

The key to safety and security in a fallen world is to stay close to the Shepherd and follow Him. Only then can you be sure the enemy will not be able to pull the wool over your eyes!

The Truth About Freedom

Fear paralyzes us from living responsibly or compels us to do that which is irresponsible. It robs us of peace and consumes our thoughts and emotions.

Sheep, by nature, are fearful creatures. But when the shepherd is around, they feel safe and secure. In the same way, fear will only control us when we lose sight of our Shepherd. Dozens of times in the Bible, God says, "Do not fear!" As you look at the following two examples from the Bible, know today that you can choose faith and not fear as you fix your eyes on Jesus:

> Do not fear, for I am with you; do not anxiously look about you, for I am your God. I will strengthen you, surely I will help you, surely I will uphold you with My righteous right hand (Isaiah 41:10).

> But now, thus says the LORD, your Creator, O Jacob, and He who formed you, O Israel, "Do not fear, for I have redeemed you; I have called you by name; you are Mine! When you pass through the waters, I will be with you; and through the rivers, they will not overflow you. When you walk through the fire, you will not be scorched, nor will the flame burn you" (Isaiah 43:1-2).

Yes, in this world you will have trouble. You can bank on that because Jesus said it would be so (see John 16:33). He also said, in that same verse, "But take courage; I have overcome the world."

Are you struggling with fear today? Know that God has not given you a spirit of fear, but instead He has given you power, love and a sound mind to overcome fear (see 2 Timothy 1:7).

Prayer for Today

My dear heavenly Father and Shepherd of my soul, thank You for taking care of me. Thank You for providing for every one of my needs—physically, mentally, emotionally, spiritually, socially and financially. Thank You that I can cast every care on You, because You indeed care for me.

In Your presence right now, I renounce the spirit of fear and forbid its operation in my life. I choose instead the power, love and sound mind of Jesus Christ, the Good Shepherd, who laid down His life for me. And I choose to walk by faith in the power of the Holy Spirit rather than succumb to the sudden terrors or chilling fears of the enemy. I refuse to fix my eyes on the problems, crimes or dangers of this world, but I lift my eyes to You, Lord, knowing that You have overcome the world. And it's in Jesus' name I pray. Amen.

DAILY SCRIPTURE READING:

ROMANS 10

Daily Journal

_____
_____
_____
_____
_____
_____
_____
_____
_____
_____

HERE COMES THE BRIDE!

When two people getting married really belong together in Christ, the wedding day becomes a wonderful event. There is nothing quite like it. There is an electricity in the air as the hour approaches. Behind the scenes, final preparations are hurriedly being made so that the bride looks her absolute best. The church is beautifully decorated with flowers. Instrumental music is setting the mood. Those in attendance, especially the bridegroom, are all in place. Everything is ready for that moment of hushed wonder and then explosive joy when the bride takes her father's arm and is led down the aisle to the groom.

One day there will be another wedding, the marriage supper of the Lamb. In heaven, when the Father presents the Bride of Christ to Jesus the Groom, the joy, pageantry and glory of that wedding will outshine all others put together.

What a glorious day that will be. Let's ask the Father to enable us to see what we can do now to prepare:

Dear heavenly Father, I anxiously look forward to the wedding of Christ to His Bride. It's almost too good to be true, like some sort of fairy tale one reads and secretly longs to happen. Yet this is not wishful thinking. It is a future reality as real as God Himself. Thank You for graciously accepting me as the Bride of Your Son, the Lord Jesus. Teach me today what You expect of me in preparation for that day. In Jesus' name I pray. Amen.

The Truth About God

God is our Father. That is the picture of our relationship with Him that we most often think about. It is also true that God, in Jesus Christ, is our spiritual Husband. It is critical we see that relationship so that we know we are not only children, but the Bride of Christ as well.

> For your husband is your Maker, whose name is the LORD of hosts; and your Redeemer is the Holy One of Israel, who is called the God of all the earth (Isaiah 54:5).

> Let us rejoice and be glad and give the glory to Him, for the marriage of the Lamb has come and His bride has made herself ready (Revelation 19:7).

One of the wonders of the heavenly wedding between Jesus and the Church is that when the Bride is presented, as glorious as she will be, all heads will turn to see the Groom. Glory to the Lamb!

As we think about Jesus as our Husband, there is an aspect of His character that naturally flows from that relationship. It is rarely spoken about, and therefore many are not aware that God is jealous:

> I am the LORD your God, who brought you out of the land of Egypt, out of the house of slavery. You shall have no other gods before Me. You shall not make for yourself an idol, or any likeness of what is in heaven above or on the earth beneath or in the water under the earth. You shall not worship them or serve them; for I, the LORD your God, am a jealous God (Exodus 20:2-5).

Exodus 34:14 even goes so far as to say "for the LORD, whose name is Jealous, is a jealous God." In other words, the very character of God is righteous jealousy.

Does that surprise you? Does this sound somehow beneath God?

Know that God never stoops to the sort of petty, catty, insecure possessiveness of humankind that characterizes sinful jealousy. The Groom's love is so intense, impassioned and filled with a holy longing to protect and purify the Church that the only way to describe it is to say that God will tolerate no rivals competing for His Bride. In that righteous respect, God is indeed a jealous God.

The Truth About You

We have already seen that the Church is the Bride of Christ. How incredible an honor it will be to be married to the Lord of the universe remains to be fully revealed, but for now a glimpse of that glory ought to breathe fresh life into the hope in your heart:

> Husbands, love your wives, just as Christ also loved the church and gave Himself up for her, so that He might sanctify her, having cleansed her by the washing of water with the word, that He might present to Himself the church in all her glory, having no spot or wrinkle or any such thing; but that she would be holy and blameless. So husbands ought also to love their own wives as their own bodies. He who loves his own wife loves himself; for no one ever hated his own flesh, but nourishes and cherishes it, just as Christ also does the church, because we are members of His body. For this cause a man shall leave his father and mother and shall be joined to his wife, and the two shall become one flesh. This mystery is great; but I am speaking with reference to Christ and the church (Ephesians 5:25-32).

Jesus did for us exactly what that passage in Ephesians is talking about. He left His Father in heaven and came to this planet to bring His Bride to Himself so that she could live in spiritual union with Him on earth now and in heaven for eternity. Such amazing grace! Such overwhelming love!

Many men feel so in love with a woman that they claim they would go to the ends of the earth for her and even die for her if necessary. What is mere talk for men became reality for Jesus, for He is moving even now throughout this world to save the Bride for whom He has already laid down His life!

The Truth About Freedom

The devil would like nothing more than to steal, kill and destroy our intimacy with Christ. The apostle Paul saw the danger of that happening and wrote:

> For I am jealous for you with a godly jealousy; for I betrothed you to one husband, that to Christ I might present you as a pure virgin. But I am afraid that, as the serpent deceived Eve by his craftiness, your minds will be led astray from the simplicity and purity of devotion to Christ (2 Corinthians 11:2-3).

When we see how committed Jesus is to loving us and how passionately He longs to make His Bride holy and pure, what should our response be? How can we continue to play the harlot with the gods of this world in the face of such jealous love? For every time we seek after anything or anyone else more than Jesus, we are committing spiritual adultery:

> You adulterous people, don't you know that friendship with the world is hatred toward God? Anyone who chooses to be a friend of the world becomes an enemy of God (James 4:4, *NIV*).

Strong words, to be sure. But would you expect anything less from a devoted Husband? Would you actually expect Him to approve of any rivals and just passively sit by and let us ruin our lives with our affairs? Never! God's love is too deep for that. So what is the solution?

James tells us later in chapter 4 that the only remedy is to come back home to the One who loves us and to cut off all involvement with the evil one who lurks behind our spiritual adultery with the world:

"God opposes the proud but gives grace to the humble." Submit yourselves, then, to God. Resist the devil, and he will flee from you. Come near to God and he will come near to you (vv. 6-8, *NIV*).

Genuine repentance may be a real battle for some. Renewing our minds and overcoming sinful habits and attachments to this world will be met with much resistance. As we do so, though, we can be assured that the Lord will lift us up in His arms and carry us back over the threshold into deep and pure intimacy with Himself once again.

Prayer for Today

Dear heavenly Father, I never quite realized how intense Your love was for me. To know that You are a jealous God reveals how much You care for me. It makes me wonder, Lord, have I guarded myself from idols [see 1 John 5:21]? Please reveal to my mind anything and everything You perceive as a real or potential rival to my loving You with all my heart and soul.

As the Lord reveals things to your mind, continue in prayer as follows:

Lord, I confess and renounce the mental and emotional affair I have had with [name the rival to Jesus]. I am so sorry that I have taken Your intense love for granted and have been seduced by the devil. I now make the heartfelt choice to turn around and come home to Your loving arms. I choose to make You my first love once again. And it's in Your name I pray. Amen.

DAILY SCRIPTURE READING:

ROMANS 11

Daily Journal

_____

_____

_____

_____

_____

_____

_____

_____

_____

_____

_____

_____

_____

_____

_____

_____

_____

_____

_____

_____

HERE COMES THE GROOM!

This world is where we live, at least for now. Yet it is not our home. No matter how good or bad things are on planet Earth, there awaits a place for us that is far better. One day we will finally be going home! What an amazing thought: Everything the Bible says about heaven is real and true. All who are in Christ are going to be with the Lord and all the saints and holy angels forever. Brother or sister in Christ, it really is going to happen!

Are you homesick for heaven? Do you miss Jesus and long to see Him face to face? Let's open this day's lesson in prayer that we might see the future with greater clarity and that we might live in the present with greater urgency:

Dear heavenly Father, Your Word says that the whole creation groans and suffers as it waits for the fullness of our adoption as Your children to take place. Deep inside me, Lord, is that same groaning and longing to be home with You. Many times, however, my love for this world dulls my hope for heaven. Purify my heart, Lord, so that I might yearn for You and my true home. I want to live in this body in such a way that pleases You. In Jesus' name I pray. Amen.

The Truth About God

Jesus came to Earth, lived, died, rose again and ascended to heaven more than 2,000 years ago. As one day rolls into the next and life goes on and on, it is easy to forget that Jesus is coming back. But He said He would return, and we have the assurance that He indeed will in God's timing!

> Do not let your heart be troubled; believe in God, believe also in Me. In My Father's house are many dwelling places; if it were not so, I would have told you; for I go to prepare a place for you. If I go and prepare a place for you, I will come again and receive you to Myself, that where I am, there you may be also (John 14:1-3).

When Jesus comes again, He will not come as the suffering servant but as the triumphant King:

> For just as the lightning comes from the east and flashes even to the west, so will the coming of the Son of Man be. But immediately after the tribulation of those days the sun will be darkened, and the moon will not give its light, and the stars will fall from the sky, and the powers of the heavens will be shaken. And then the sign of the Son of Man will appear in the sky, and then all the tribes of the earth will mourn, and they will see the Son of Man coming on the clouds of the sky with power and great glory. And He will send forth His angels with a great trumpet and they will gather together His elect from the four winds, from one end of the sky to the other (Matthew 24:27,29-31).

Jesus will come with great power and glory. Every eye will see Him, and every ear will hear the angel's trumpet blast as He gathers His people to Himself. For indeed, Jesus came the first time to die for the sins of the world. The next time, He is coming to take His children home. That ought to quiet our troubled hearts.

And just as it is destined that men die only once, and after that comes judgment, so also Christ died only once as an offering for the sins of many people; and he will come again, but not to deal again with our sins. This time he will come bringing salvation to all those who are eagerly and patiently waiting for him (Hebrews 9:27-28, *TLB*).

The Truth About You

Unless you are homeless, you live in some kind of a house or apartment. However, your true home is in heaven because you belong to Jesus Christ. This is not just spiritual talk but a critical truth that will determine how we live on this earth. Consider the following Scripture verses:

For our citizenship is in heaven, from which also we eagerly wait for a Savior, the Lord Jesus Christ; who will transform the body of our humble state into conformity with the body of His glory, by the exertion of the power that He has even to subject all things to Himself (Philippians 3:20-21).

All [the Old Testament heroes] died in faith, without receiving the promises, but having seen them and having welcomed them from a distance, and having confessed that they were strangers and exiles on the earth. For those who say such things make it clear that they are seeking a country of their own. And indeed if they had been thinking of that country from which they went out, they would have had opportunity to return. But as it is, they desire a better country, that is, a heavenly one. Therefore God is not ashamed to be called their God; for He has prepared a city for them (Hebrews 11:13-16).

Too often our lives are cluttered with the goodies of this world, and our love and devotion to the coming King diminish. It is a real possibility and danger to become so enamored with the gifts God gives us that we have little desire for the Giver. We end up being so comfortable on Earth that we have little or no longing or yearning for our real home.

Some would say that those who long for the return of Jesus are so heavenly minded that they are no earthly good, but that is not necessarily true. The reality is that so many Christians are so earthly minded that they are no heavenly good!

Are you eagerly awaiting the return of the Savior? Do you want to see Him face to face in the same way the disciples did when they gazed at Christ's ascension into heaven? That is what the Bible says we should be like, for we are indeed aliens and strangers on this earth. But, praise God, we are citizens of heaven right now!

The Truth About Freedom

To live in freedom in an increasingly materialistic culture, we must renounce the love of money that is the root of all sorts of evil. We also must embrace contentment with what God has given us in life, even if things are tough (see 1 Timothy 6:6-10). Moses is a worthy example to follow:

> By faith Moses, when he had grown up, refused to be called the son of Pharaoh's daughter, choosing rather to endure ill-treatment with the people of God than to enjoy the passing pleasures of sin, considering the reproach of Christ greater riches than the treasures of Egypt; for he was looking to the reward (Hebrews 11:24-26).

Only those who have loosened their grip on this world are truly free to minister in it. Only those who are waiting eagerly for life in the next world are truly free to live holy lives in the present.

But you are a chosen race, a royal priesthood, a holy nation, a people for God's own possession, so that you may proclaim the excellencies of Him who has called you out of darkness into His marvelous light; for you once were not a people, but now you are the people of God; you had not received mercy, but now you have received mercy. Beloved, I urge you as aliens and strangers to abstain from fleshly lusts which wage war against the soul (1 Peter 2:9-11).

But do not let this one fact escape your notice, beloved, that with the Lord one day is like a thousand years, and a thousand years like one day. The Lord is not slow about His promise [to return], as some count slowness, but is patient toward you, not wishing for any to perish but for all to come to repentance. But the day of the Lord will come like a thief, in which the heavens will pass away with a roar and the elements will be destroyed with intense heat, and the earth and its works will be burned up. Since all these things are to be destroyed in this way, what sort of people ought you to be in holy conduct and godliness, looking for and hastening the coming of the day of God, because of which the heavens will be destroyed by burning, and the elements will melt with intense heat! But according to His promise we are looking for new heavens and a new earth, in which righteousness dwells (2 Peter 3:8-13).

Prayer for Today

Dear heavenly Father, thank You for reminding me that Your Son is coming again to take me to my true home. Please open my eyes to the ways I have loved this world and its value system. Prune back the thorns in my life, Lord, that choke out the Word and make it unfruitful. I renounce my preoccupation with the worries of this world, the deceitfulness of riches, and my desire for material things. I want to be able to say with all my heart, "For to me, to live is Christ and to die is gain" [Philippians 1:21]. I choose now to return to a simple and pure devotion to Christ and an eager longing to see Him. In the name of Jesus, my Coming King, I pray. Amen.

DAILY SCRIPTURE READING:

ROMANS 12

Daily Journal

_____
_____
_____
_____
_____
_____
_____
_____
_____
_____
_____
_____
_____
_____
_____
_____
_____
_____

Counselors warn us of the times when we are the most vulnerable to the sins of the flesh. Such times can be illustrated by the acrostic BLASTED. Be especially aware during times when you are:

Bored
Lonely
Angry
Self-pitying
Tired
Extra-stressed
Depressed

These are the times when our guard tends to be down. We can justify an excursion into sin by believing it will relieve the pressure.

The good news is that you don't have to do that. Romans 6:11 urges you to "consider yourselves to be dead to sin, but alive to God in Christ Jesus." We are to consider this to be true because it is! We do not have to give in to sin anymore. It is no longer our master, for we are now under grace (see v. 14).

We have the responsibility to live above sin. We must choose to walk by the Spirit and not fulfill the lusts of the flesh (see Galatians 5:16). Knowing that the lusts of the flesh wage war against our souls should motivate us to abstain from those destructive urges (see 1 Peter 2:11).

If you are serious about moving beyond the revolving door of "sin, confess, sin, confess" only to eventually just give up and give in to sin, then pray as follows:

Dear heavenly Father, You have told me to put on the Lord Jesus Christ and make no provision for the flesh in regard to its lusts. I confess, however, that I have many times given in to temptation and sinned. I thank You that I am forgiven in Christ, but I want to break any holds that the enemy has over me because of my fleshly sin. I come to You now, asking You to show me specifically the deeds of the flesh I have committed so that through confession, I might experience Your cleansing and freedom from bondage. In Jesus' holy name I pray. Amen.

Mark 7:20-23, Romans 1:18-32, Galatians 5:19-21,26 and Ephesians 4:14-32 provide insight into some of the fleshly sins you may need to confess:

sexual immorality	gossip	petty doctrinal
living for pleasure	greed	battles
witchcraft	arrogance	lying
strife	adultery	hurtful words
angry outbursts	lustful thoughts	slander
divisions	idolatry	homosexuality
envy	hatred	murder
lewd parties	jealousy	disobedience to
stealing	arguments	authority
festering anger	drunkenness	pride

For each area the Lord surfaces in your life, pray the following prayer of confession and renunciation:

Dear Lord, Your Spirit and Your Word have shown me that I am guilty of the fleshly sins of [name each specific sin]. I thank You for Your forgiveness and cleansing. With all my heart, I repent of these sins and renounce them now, taking back the ground the enemy gained in me through my disobedience. I present to You once again all the parts of my body that have been involved in sin, namely [name the specific parts of your body]. Strengthen me by Your Holy Spirit to obey You. In Jesus' holy name I pray. Amen.

19

A FRIEND OF SINNERS

Why is it that so many unbelievers could not care less about Christ? Why are so few churches seeing a real movement of sinners being saved? These are disturbing questions when you understand that God has called us to be the salt of the earth and the light of the world (see Matthew 5:13-14).

Certainly the selfishly ambitious pursuit of power and greedy love of money and material possessions distract many from seeking Christ. But the influx of people into New Age and metaphysical religions testifies that there is a yearning in people's hearts for a deeper reality in life. Could it be that most people view Jesus as being old-fashioned and irrelevant to their fast-paced lives? Could it also be that most Christians have missed the boat about how to influence their world? Only God has the answers to these important questions, and He will indeed open our eyes as we ask Him in prayer:

> *Dear heavenly Father, I know that You have not saved me and set me free just to blend comfortably into the culture around me nor to sit complacently in a church pew. You have called me to be Your witness, and I know it is only by Your Spirit's empowering that I can do that. Please reveal to me Your heart for the lost, Lord Jesus, and make me like You. It's in Your name I pray. Amen.*

The Truth About God

Have you ever wondered what Jesus would look like, dress like, talk like and act like if He had decided to come to twenty-first-century America rather than first-century Israel? Well, one thing is for sure: He would not have been some stuffy, pompous, hide-in-the-office kind of guy. It may amaze you, but when Jesus walked on Earth, He was criticized for partying with sinners!

> Then it happened that as Jesus was reclining at the table in the house [of Matthew the tax collector], behold, many tax collectors and sinners came and were dining with Jesus and His disciples. When the Pharisees saw this, they said to His disciples, "Why is your Teacher eating with the tax collectors and sinners?" But when He heard this, He said, "It is not those who are healthy who need a physician, but those who are sick. But go and learn what this means: 'I desire compassion, and not sacrifice,' for I did not come to call the righteous, but sinners" (Matthew 9:10-13).

Jesus was so down-to-earth and in touch with people and life that He was accused of being "a gluttonous man and a drunkard, a friend of tax collectors and sinners!" (Matthew 11:19).

A friend of sinners—I bet Jesus liked that title, because that is exactly what He came to be. He wept over the city of Jerusalem, because they would not open their hearts to Him (see Matthew 23:37-39; Luke 13:34). He was saddened when He looked at the crowds of people and saw how distressed and downcast they were (see Matthew 9:35-38). Jesus was moved with compassion over the deep, deep needs of the people around Him and greatly grieved over the hardness of heart of those who rejected Him.

So that is why He went to the cross—to turn lost sinners into redeemed saints:

Now all these things are from God, who reconciled us to Himself [made us His friends] through Christ and gave us the ministry of reconciliation, namely, that God was in Christ reconciling the world to Himself, not counting their trespasses against them (2 Corinthians 5:18-19).

Is that the picture of an irrelevant, uncaring God? Not at all. It is rather the picture of an involved and compassionate Father who sacrificed His greatest love to meet our greatest need.

The Truth About You

In Christ, you and I have been reconciled to God. We are no longer enemies but friends with Him.

But God showed his great love for us by sending Christ to die for us while we were still sinners. And since by his blood he did all this for us as sinners, how much more will he do for us now that he has declared us not guilty? Now he will save us from all of God's wrath to come. And since, when we were his enemies, we were brought back to God by the death of his Son, what blessings he must have for us now that we are his friends, and he is living within us! (Romans 5:8-10, *TLB*).

One of the hallmarks among friends is that they talk together about important things. Our relationship with Jesus is no different. He has chosen to confide in us what is really on His heart:

No longer do I call you slaves, for the slave does not know what his master is doing; but I have called you friends, for all things that I have heard from My Father I have made known to you (John 15:15).

So what is on the Father's heart that our best friend Jesus wants to make known to us? God wants us to know that He chose us and appointed us to go and bear fruit that would remain (see v. 16). We have a definite role to play in the Father's plan of reaching a dying world:

For the love of Christ controls us, having concluded this, that one died for all, therefore all died; and He died for all, that they who live might no longer live for themselves, but for Him who died and rose again on their behalf. Therefore, we are ambassadors for Christ, as though God were making an appeal through us; we beg you on behalf of Christ, be reconciled to God (2 Corinthians 5:14-15,20).

Jesus, the friend of sinners, is still reaching out to them through us. We are His feet to go, His arms to embrace, His mouth to proclaim the good news that God wants people to receive His Son and be His friends. The Bible says we are ambassadors. That is the calling of every child of God. The question is, Are we faithfully representing the King in this world?

The Truth About Freedom

Once we have been saved and set free by the grace and power of God, it is the most natural thing in the world for us to want to help others. Sometimes, however, we are not free to be Christ's bold, Spirit-empowered witnesses (see Acts 1:8), because of our fear of people.

The stakes are too high, however, to withhold the words of life from others who are on a runaway train bound for the lake of fire. Is it not the depth of selfishness to fearfully preserve our reputation or friendship with others while robbing them of the chance to become friends with God?

Paul's child in the faith, Timothy, apparently struggled with the fear of people. His mentor's words of encouragement ought to encourage us as well:

For God has not given us a spirit of timidity, but of power and love and discipline. Therefore do not be ashamed of the testimony of our Lord or of me His prisoner, but join with me in suffering for the gospel according to the power of God (2 Timothy 1:7-8).

For this reason I endure all things for the sake of those who are chosen, that they also may obtain the salvation which is in Christ Jesus and with it eternal glory (2 Timothy 2:10).

I solemnly charge you in the presence of God and of Christ Jesus, who is to judge the living and the dead, and by His appearing and His kingdom: preach the word; be ready in season and out of season; reprove, rebuke, exhort, with great patience and instruction. But you, be sober in all things, endure hardship, do the work of an evangelist, fulfill your ministry (2 Timothy 4:1-2,5).

Prayer for Today

Dear heavenly Father, Your compassionate heart for the lost is so great. You drew me to Yourself, and I don't want to keep the words of life to myself anymore. Your heart is so big that You desire that no one should perish. Therefore, I receive my call as an ambassador for Christ, and I pray that You would liberate and empower me for a ministry of reconciliation. May my heart be broken over the lost souls around me, and may I do the work of an evangelist, fulfilling the ministry You have given me. In the name of Jesus, the friend of sinners, I pray. Amen.

DAILY SCRIPTURE READING:

ROMANS 13

Daily Journal

_____
_____
_____
_____
_____
_____
_____
_____
_____
_____
_____
_____
_____
_____
_____
_____
_____
_____
_____
_____
_____
_____
_____
_____
_____
_____
_____
_____
_____

20

BODY LIFE

The covenant love relationship that exists between God and His people is so intimate, dynamic and mysterious that no one illustration from life can fully explain it. In this devotional, we have seen that God is our Father and we are His children; Jesus is our Shepherd and we are His sheep; He is also our Husband and we are the Bride of Christ; Jesus is the Vine and we are the branches; and so on.

But there's still more! God didn't want us to miss the reality of how we are connected with other believers in Christ, so He has revealed another relationship between Jesus and His Church: He is the Head and we are the Body of Christ.

Dear heavenly Father, I thank You for the brothers and sisters in Christ You have put into my life. They are such an encouragement to me. There are times though, Lord, when my flesh rears its ugly head, and I give in to anger, resentment, envy, jealousy or strife. All these things are so divisive, Lord. Teach me Your role as Head of the Church, and my role in Your Body to preserve the unity of the Spirit in the bond of peace. In Jesus' name I pray. Amen.

The Truth About God

The books of Ephesians and Colossians are primers when it comes to understanding who we are in Christ and who Christ is in us. Therefore, we will turn there to see what Paul said about Jesus' role over the Church:

> [The Father] put all things in subjection under [Christ's] feet, and gave Him as head over all things to the church, which is His body, the fullness of Him who fills all in all (Ephesians 1:22-23).

> [Christ] is before all things, and in Him all things hold together. He is also head of the body, the church; and He is the beginning, the firstborn from the dead, so that He Himself will come to have first place in everything (Colossians 1:17-18).

Just as the head of our physical body directs the rest of the body and all its workings, so Christ, the Head of the Church, regulates His Body. At least, that is the way it is supposed to work.

Jesus ought to have first place in everything, because He is head over the whole Church. In Revelation 1-3, we see how Christ exercises leadership over individual congregations in His Church. He encourages, commends, reproves, warns and executes judgment and rewards. In a vision given to John, Jesus' words teach us of His headship over His Church:

> Do not be afraid; I am the first and the last, and the living One; and I was dead, and behold, I am alive forevermore, and I have the keys of death and of Hades. As for the mystery of the seven stars which you saw in My right hand, and the seven golden lampstands: the seven stars are the angels of the seven churches, and the seven lampstands are the seven churches (Revelation 1:17-18,20).

Christ indeed is the Head of the Church, being the Savior of the Body (see Ephesians 5:23).

The Truth About You

Much of Paul's instruction in 1 Corinthians speaks to our relationship with Christ and to each other as members of His Body. We are different but united:

> For even as the body is one and yet has many members, and all the members of the body, though they are many, are one body, so also is Christ. For by one Spirit we were all baptized into one body, whether Jews or Greeks, whether slaves or free, and we were all made to drink of one Spirit. For the body is not one member, but many (12:12-14).

The unity of the Body of Christ is important. We come from a variety of backgrounds—denominationally, economically and culturally—but we are all part of the same Body. This unity sets the stage for appreciating one another's diversity of gifts and roles in the Body.

Just as a foot or an ear would be wrong to have an inferiority complex because it is not an eye, so believers should not feel unimportant because they are not as visibly gifted or well known as others. All gifts are important to the healthy functioning of the whole (see 1 Corinthians 12:15-17).

It should encourage us to know that God is the One who has chosen and designated our individual gifts, talents and ministries (see vv. 4-6). This is not primarily for our own blessing but for the good of the whole Body (see v. 7) and for God's own pleasure (see v. 18).

For this same reason, we should not feel superior to others. One who puts others down in the Body because they seem to be weaker or less gifted is acting contrary to Christ. We all need each other!

> But God has so composed the body, giving more abundant honor to that member which lacked, so that there

may be no division in the body, but that the members should have the same care for one another. And if one member suffers, all the members suffer with it; if one member is honored, all the members rejoice with it. Now you are Christ's body, and individually members of it (1 Corinthians 12:24-27).

God gifts every believer in Christ in some way for furthering His kingdom and for building up the Body. Therefore, we should rejoice in the significant way we, as well as others, can contribute to the whole. Our responsibility is to submit to the Head of the Church. When we do so, the Body of Christ, like a well-trained athlete or soldier, functions as a whole to the glory of God!

The Truth About Freedom

The devil knows there is no more formidable enemy than the Body of Christ praying and serving together under the direct headship of Christ. Therefore, his strategy is always to divide and conquer. If he succeeds, the Body of Christ is not free to make any significant impact for the kingdom of God. We must find our place in the Body of Christ and seek to build up one another in love.

If I speak with the tongues of men and of angels, but do not have love, I have become a noisy gong or a clanging cymbal. And if I have the gift of prophecy, and know all mysteries and all knowledge; and if I have all faith, so as to remove mountains, but do not have love, I am nothing. And if I give all my possessions to feed the poor, and if I surrender my body to be burned, but do not have love, it profits me nothing (1 Corinthians 13:1-3).

But speaking the truth in love, we are to grow up in all aspects into Him who is the head, even Christ, from whom the whole body, being fitted and held together by that what every joint supplies, according to the proper working of each individual part, causes the growth of the body for the building up of itself in love (Ephesians 4:15-16).

Prayer for Today

Dear heavenly Father, I bow my knee before Jesus, the Head of the Church. I renounce all foolish comparison with others [see 2 Corinthians 10:12], and put away all strife, jealousy, angry temper, disputes, slanders, gossip, arrogance and disturbances [see 2 Corinthians 12:20]. I refuse to be a member of the devil's wrecking crew. I choose from this day forward to be part of God's building crew and to speak the truth in love. I thank You for how You have gifted me, and I pray You would guide and empower me in the use of those abilities. I also rejoice in how You have gifted others and pray for Your anointing on them as well. In the name of Jesus I pray. Amen.

DAILY SCRIPTURE READING:

ROMANS 14

Daily Journal

_____

_____

_____

_____

_____

_____

_____

21

IN HIS MAJESTY'S
SERVICE

This is the last lesson in our three-week journey of better understanding God, ourselves and our walk with God in freedom. However, it is meant to be just the beginning—the beginning of a godly lifestyle of eagerly pursuing God. We encourage you to follow through to the end of this devotional guide, including Freedom Refresher 7 and Focal Point (and a review of the Steps to Freedom in Christ, if you haven't already done that). Together, those exercises provide a fitting conclusion to this study and will help you maintain your spiritual freedom and enable you to move on to maturity in Christ.

Let's open this final day's study by asking the Author of the Word of God to instruct us:

Dear heavenly Father, I thank You for all You have been doing in my life these past three weeks. Drinking deeply from Your fountain of living waters has both satisfied me and made me thirsty for more. Continue, Lord, making me lie down in green pastures, leading me beside still waters and restoring my soul. I want to walk with You all the days of my life. So once again, please open my eyes and heart to see You today as You are and to understand from Your Word what I need to know to walk in freedom. In the name of Jesus, who sets me free, I pray. Amen.

The Truth About God

"The LORD, He is God! The LORD, He is God!" This was the cry of the people of God on Mount Carmel after they had fallen on their faces before His awesome power. In response to a simple prayer from the prophet Elijah, fire from God had fallen on the sacrifice. In so acting, God declared that He, not Baal, was in charge (see 1 Kings 18:20-40, especially v. 39). Throughout Scripture and history, that same proclamation has resounded: "The Lord is God!"

The preaching of the prophet Isaiah rebuked the crass idolatry that was rampant in Israel in that day. His book is filled with glorious truths of God's lordship:

"You are My witnesses," declares the LORD, "and My servant whom I have chosen, so that you may know and believe Me and understand that I am He. Before Me there was no God formed, and there will be none after Me. I, even I, am the LORD; and there is no savior besides Me. It is I who have declared and saved and proclaimed, and there was no strange god among you; so you are My witnesses," declares the LORD, "and I am God. Even from eternity I am He; and there is none who can deliver out of My hand; I act and who can reverse it?" (Isaiah 43:10-13).

The message is clear. The Lord, Yahweh, is God. He is the Lord of the entire universe. There has never been any other God, and there never will be. No one else can save. No one can stop God from doing what He intends to do. No one can change His mighty works. He is the supreme and sovereign Lord of all!

Jesus often offended the religious leaders of His day, but one day He really exposed the true nature of their hearts. The Pharisees were boasting about being Abraham's children, yet Jesus called them on the carpet for their murderous thoughts.

He exposed the truth that their hearts betrayed them, showing that they were of their father the devil, not Abraham.

> "Your father Abraham rejoiced to see My day, and he saw it and was glad." The Jews therefore said to Him, "You are not yet fifty years old, and have You seen Abraham?" Jesus said to them, "Truly, truly, I say to you, before Abraham was born, I am." Therefore they picked up stones to throw at Him, but Jesus hid Himself and went out of the temple (John 8:56-59).

Did you notice the verb tense of Jesus' reply? "Before Abraham was born, *I am*." Jesus was declaring Himself to be the Lord who spoke to Moses in the burning bush. That was where God gave us His name, "I AM" (see Exodus 3:4). That's why the Jews picked up stones to kill Him. They knew He was claiming to be God Almighty. And He is! Our heavenly Father has "seated Him at His right hand in the heavenly places, far above all rule and authority and power and dominion, and every name that is named, not only in this age but also in the one to come" (Ephesians 1:20-21). "Hallelujah! For the Lord our God, the Almighty, reigns" (Revelation 19:6). Hail, Lord Jesus, King of kings and Lord of lords, who has all authority in heaven and earth (see Matthew 28:18)!

The Truth About You

Jesus is at the right hand of the Father in heaven. "Right hand" refers to the position of authority, and in Jesus' case, that means *all* authority. That means that the devil, demons and evil men can only do that which Jesus allows them to do. They are on a leash, held fast in the grip of Jesus the King.

What does Jesus' position at the right hand of the Father have to do with us? It has everything to do with us because we are "in Christ," as the following Scripture teaches:

But God, being rich in mercy, because of His great love with which He loved us, even when we were dead in our transgressions, made us alive together with Christ (by grace you have been saved), and raised us up with Him, and seated us with Him in the heavenly places in Christ Jesus (Ephesians 2:4-6).

We are eternally alive in Christ. Our souls are in union with Him. Therefore, when Christ died, we died. When He rose from the dead, we rose with Him. When Jesus was raised to heaven to sit at God's right hand—you guessed it—we were raised to sit with Him!

So where are we in relation to the Father right now? We are seated with Christ at God's right hand. What does this mean? It means that the Church, the Body of Christ, has the authority to do His will! We are to exercise Christ's authority on earth.

Individually, that means you and I have the right to tell the devil to take his evil hands off us, our families, our homes, our ministries, and so on. Corporately, the Church has the right to bind the strong man, Satan, and take from him his spoils—the captive souls of men and women!

The Truth About Freedom

Many Christians perceive themselves as weak, inadequate, un-important victims: *Woe am I, an ineffective miserable sinner in the Body of Christ.*

This "worm theology" is dishonoring to the God who has raised us up to sit with Christ and who has called us heirs of God and coheirs with Christ (see Romans 8:17). Jesus has set us free, but He did not intend for us to wring our hands, moaning and complaining and sitting passively by while evil rules. He has liberated us from sin's power so that we can exercise our God-given authority by praying, preaching the gospel and setting captives free. Paul gives us a taste of this in Romans 5:17:

For if by the transgression of the one, death reigned through the one, much more those who receive the abundance of grace and of the gift of righteousness will reign in life through the One, Jesus Christ.

Make no mistake about it. Reigning with Jesus on earth may be costly. It cost Jesus His life. We must be willing to lay down our lives for the brethren as well (see 1 John 3:16). When we mature to that degree of love, the devil has lost all control over us, and we are truly free!

Now the salvation, and the power, and the kingdom of our God and the authority of His Christ have come, for the accuser of our brethren [Satan] has been thrown down, he who accuses them before our God day and night. And they overcame him because of the blood of the Lamb and because of the word of their testimony, and they did not love their life even when faced with death (Revelation 12:10-11).

Prayer for Today

Dear heavenly Father, I worship You as Lord. You are my God and the God of all eternity. Your Son, Jesus Christ, is the King of all kings and Lord of all lords. And, Jesus, I bow before You and submit to You as my Lord. Thank You, Father, for raising me up with Christ to sit at Your right hand of all authority. Teach me how to reign in life through You. Equip me as a prayer warrior, as an evangelist and as a liberator of the captive souls around me. You have told me, O Lord of the hosts of heavenly angels, that it is not by my own might or power but by Your Spirit [see Zechariah 4:6]. Bring me, Lord, to the point where I can even let go of this earthly life, if necessary, for Your kingdom and glory. In Jesus' name I ask it all. Amen.

DAILY SCRIPTURE READING:

ROMANS 15–16

Daily Journal

_____
_____
_____
_____
_____
_____
_____
_____
_____
_____
_____
_____
_____
_____
_____
_____
_____
_____
_____
_____
_____
_____
_____
_____
_____
_____
_____
_____
_____

FREEDOM
REFRESHER
={SEVEN}=

This final Freedom Refresher, like Step Seven of the Steps to Freedom in Christ, addresses the issue of how our predisposition toward certain sins can be passed down through family lines and, consequently, how to walk free from those influences. It also brings up the subject of how we can come under spiritual attack. Both of these concerns can have a profound effect on our walk of freedom, though it is possible to be largely unaware of their powerful influence. It requires discernment from the Spirit of God to detect the presence and control of these sins and attacks. Will you join us in a prayer for such discernment?

Dear heavenly Father, I know that I am a new creation in Christ. I am no longer in Adam; I am now in Christ. I am part of the family of God with all the accompanying blessings and responsibilities. But I also recognize that just as the flesh can still assert control if I let it, so can the sins of the fathers. Lord, reveal to my mind the sins and iniquities that I picked up from my earthly family [see 1 Peter 1:18]. Reveal to me the ways in which my family, my possessions, my ministry or my personal life have come under attack by demonic forces. I need and pray for Your supernatural discernment in these matters. I want to be free from these ungodly influences so that I can walk in the fullness of freedom in You. In the name of Jesus, in whom are hidden all the treasures of wisdom and knowledge, I pray. Amen.

As the Lord brings specific sins of the fathers or demonic influences to your mind, list them on the lines provided on the following page. You will be specifically renouncing them in the declaration at the end of this section.

Sins of the Fathers: Attacks:

_____	_____
_____	_____
_____	_____
_____	_____
_____	_____
_____	_____
_____	_____
_____	_____
_____	_____
_____	_____

In the name and authority of the Lord Jesus Christ, I here and now reject and disown all the sins of my ancestors. I specifically renounce the sins of [specifically name each sin you listed under "Sins of the Fathers"]. As one who has been delivered from the domain of darkness and transferred into the kingdom of God's Son, I cancel out all demonic working that has been passed down to me through my family. I choose to live my life in Christ.

As one who has been crucified and raised with Jesus Christ and who sits with Him in heavenly places, I renounce all satanic assignments that are directed toward me, my family, my possessions or my ministry. I cancel out [specifically name each attack you listed under "Attacks"] and any other means by which Satan and his workers have targeted me.

I reject any and all ways in which Satan may claim ownership of me. I belong to the Lord Jesus Christ, who purchased me with His shed blood. I declare myself to be fully and eternally signed over and committed to the Lord Jesus Christ. Amen!

FOCAL POINT

Now that you have completed this 21-day devotional guide, we want to help you stay focused in your efforts to maintain your freedom in Christ. During these last three weeks, we trust the Lord spoke to you, revealing lies that you had believed about God and yourself, giving you greater wisdom in how to live freely in Christ. We trust He has also begun to replace those lies with the truth that sets you free.

Because it is so easy to slip back into old habit patterns of believing and behaving, we have designed this project as a prayer reminder to help you to continue to renew your mind. The apostle Paul taught that the key to changing your life is changing your mind:

> Therefore I urge you, brethren, by the mercies of God, to present your bodies a living and holy sacrifice, acceptable to God, which is your spiritual service of worship. And do not be conformed to this world, but be transformed by the renewing of your mind, so that you may prove what the will of God is, that which is good and acceptable and perfect (Romans 12:1-2).

Before we proceed any further, read the following prayer silently and then, if it expresses your heart, sincerely pray it aloud to God:

> *Dear heavenly Father, I have lived too much of my life in my own strength, for my own selfish reasons. I want no more of such an existence. I want to live Christ's life and no other. I choose this day to present every part of my body to You in*

worship and service. I choose also to renounce this world's value system and instead choose to have my mind renewed by Your truth. I know that by so doing my life will be transformed, and I will know in my heart that Your will is always what is good and best for me. In Jesus' name I pray. Amen.

Before filling out the "Personal Prayer Action Plan," we encourage you to take a few minutes and prayerfully skim back over this devotional guide. This will prompt your memory to recall the things that were most meaningful for you in those lessons. Looking over the "Daily Journal" entries should help as well.

When you have completed that review, ask the Lord to help you respond to the following questions. Use the space provided after each question to jot down your thoughts.

What are the most significant lies I had believed about God, myself and living free in Christ? (Consult "The Truth About God," "The Truth About You" and "The Truth About Freedom" sections.)

_____

_____

_____

_____

_____

_____

_____

What are the most important truths I need to choose to believe about God, myself and living free in Christ? (Consult "The Truth About God," "The Truth About You" and "The Truth About Freedom" sections.)

_____

_____

_____

_____

_____

_____

_____

_____

What are the most critical decisions of obedience that I need to make to maintain freedom and move on in spiritual maturity? (Consult the "Prayer for Today" section and read over your daily journal entries.)

_____

_____

_____

_____

_____

_____

_____

Now, having jotted down your initial answers to each question, select the three most crucial issues under each:

The Most Significant Lies I Believed . . .

About God:
1. _____
2. _____
3. _____

About Myself:
1. _____
2. _____
3. _____

About Freedom:

1. _____
2. _____
3. _____

The Most Important Truths I Need to Believe . . .

About God:

1. _____
2. _____
3. _____

About Myself:

1. _____
2. _____
3. _____

About Freedom:

1. _____
2. _____
3. _____

The Three Most Critical Decisions I Need to Make:

1. _____
2. _____
3. _____

The following "Personal Prayer Action Plan" chart is designed for you to fill out, using the lists you have just completed. You will probably want to summarize and shorten your statements before placing them in the chart. Feel free to tear the "Personal Prayer Action Plan" out of this devotional guide and carry it with you. You might want to keep it in your Bible for easy access and ready reference.

We encourage you to make a daily habit of reading through this plan out loud for the next 40 days. Let it become the basis for your personal prayer times with God. As the Lord leads you, it can also be something to share with trustworthy family members or friends who will commit themselves to praying for you during these next 40 days and beyond.

May the Lord indeed give you perseverance and joy as you develop the lifelong habit of walking with God by faith in the power of the Holy Spirit. God bless you!

PERSONAL PRAYER ACTION PLAN

I renounce the lie about God . . .	I announce the truth about God . . .
1.	1.
2.	2.
3.	3.
I make the decision in the power of the Holy Spirit to . . .	

PERSONAL PRAYER ACTION PLAN

I renounce the lie about myself . . .	I announce the truth about myself . . .
1.	1.
2.	2.
3.	3.
I make the decision in the power of the Holy Spirit to . . .	

PERSONAL PRAYER ACTION PLAN

I renounce the lie about living free in Christ . . .	I announce the truth about living free in Christ . . .
1.	1.
2.	2.
3.	3.
I make the decision in the power of the Holy Spirit to . . .	

STEPS TO FREEDOM IN CHRIST

It is my deep conviction that the finished work of Jesus Christ and the presence of God in our lives are the only means by which we can resolve our personal and spiritual conflicts. Christ in us is our only hope (see Colossians 1:27), and He alone can meet our deepest needs of life: acceptance, identity, security and significance. The discipleship counseling process on which these steps are based should not be understood as just another counseling technique that we learn. It is an encounter with God. He is the Wonderful Counselor. He is the One who grants repentance that leads to a knowledge of the truth that sets us free (see 2 Timothy 2:25-26).

The Steps to Freedom in Christ do not set you free. *Who* sets you free is Christ, and *what* sets you free is your response to Him in repentance and faith. These steps are just a tool to help you submit to God and resist the devil (see James 4:7). Then you can start living a fruitful life by abiding in Christ and becoming the person He created you to be. Many Christians will be able to work through these steps on their own and discover the wonderful freedom that Christ purchased for them on the cross. Then they will experience the peace of God that surpasses all comprehension, and it shall guard their hearts and their minds (see Philippians 4:7, *NASB*).

Before You Begin

The chances of that happening and the possibility of maintaining that freedom will be greatly enhanced if you read *Victory Over the Darkness* and *The Bondage Breaker* first. Many Christians in the western world need to understand the reality of the spiritual world and our relationship to it. Some can't read these books or even the Bible with comprehension because of the battle that is going on for their minds. They will need the assistance of others who have been trained. The theology and practical process of discipleship counseling is given in my book *Helping Others Find Freedom in Christ* and in the accompanying *Training Manual and Study Guide* and Video Training Program. The book attempts to biblically integrate the reality of the spiritual and the natural world so that we can have a whole answer for a whole person. In doing so, we cannot polarize into psychotherapeutic ministries that ignore the reality of the spiritual world or attempt some kind of deliverance ministry that ignores developmental issues and human responsibility.

You May Need Help

Ideally, it would be best if everyone had a trusted friend, pastor or counselor who would help them go through this process because it is just applying the wisdom of James 5:16: "Therefore confess your sins to each other and pray for each other so that you may be healed. The prayer of a righteous man is powerful and effective." Another person can prayerfully support you by providing objective counsel. I have had the privilege of helping many Christian leaders who could not process this on their own. Many Christian groups all over the world are using this approach in many languages with incredible results because the Lord desires for all to come to repentance (see 2 Peter 3:9), and to know the truth that sets us free in Christ (see John 8:32).

Appropriating and Maintaining Freedom

Christ has set us free through His victory over sin and death on the cross. However, appropriating our freedom in Christ through repentance and faith and maintaining our life of freedom in Christ are two different issues. It was for freedom that Christ set us free, but we have been warned not to return to a yoke of slavery that is legalism in this context (see Galatians 5:1) or to turn our freedom into an opportunity for the flesh (see Galatians 5:13). Establishing people free in Christ makes it possible for them to walk by faith according to what God says is true, to live by the power of the Holy Spirit and to not carry out the desires of the flesh (see Galatians 5:16). The true Christian life avoids both legalism and license.

If you are not experiencing freedom, it may be because you have not stood firm in the faith or actively taken your place in Christ. It is every Christian's responsibility to do whatever is necessary to maintain a right relationship with God and mankind. Your eternal destiny is not at stake. God will never leave you nor forsake you (see Hebrews 13:5), but your daily victory is at stake if you fail to claim and maintain your position in Christ.

Your Position in Christ

You are not a helpless victim caught between two nearly equal but opposite heavenly superpowers. Satan is a deceiver. Only God is omnipotent, omnipresent and omniscient. Sometimes the reality of sin and the presence of evil may seem more real than the presence of God, but that's part of Satan's deception. Satan is a defeated foe and we are in Christ. A true knowledge of God and knowing our identity and position in Christ are the greatest determinants of our mental health. A false concept of God, a distorted understanding of who we are as children of God, and the misplaced deification of Satan are the greatest contributors to mental illness.

Many of our illnesses are psychosomatic. When these issues are resolved in Christ, our physical bodies will function better and we will experience greater health. Other problems are clearly physical and we need the services of the medical profession. Please consult your physician for medical advice and the prescribing of medication. We are both spiritual and physical beings who need the services of both the church and the medical profession.

Winning the Battle for Your Mind

The battle is for our minds, which is the control center of all that we think and do. The opposing thoughts you may experience as you go through these steps can control you only if you believe them. If you are working through these steps alone, don't be deceived by any lying, intimidating thoughts in your mind. If a trusted pastor or counselor is helping you find your freedom in Christ, he or she must have your cooperation. You must share any thoughts you are having in opposition to what you are attempting to do. As soon as you expose the lie, the power of Satan is broken. The only way that you can lose control in this process is if you pay attention to a deceiving spirit and believe a lie.

You Must Choose

The following procedure is a means of resolving personal and spiritual conflicts that have kept you from experiencing the freedom and victory Christ purchased for you on the cross. Your freedom will be the result of what *you* choose to believe, confess, forgive, renounce and forsake. No one can do that for you. The battle for your mind can only be won as you personally choose truth. As you go through this process, understand that Satan is under no obligation to obey your thoughts. Only God has complete knowledge of your mind because He is omniscient—all-knowing. So we can submit to God inwardly, but we need to resist the devil by reading aloud each prayer and by verbally renouncing, forgiving, confessing, and so forth.

This process of reestablishing our freedom in Christ is nothing more than a fierce moral inventory and a rock-solid commitment to truth. It is the first step in the continuing process of discipleship. There is no such thing as instant maturity. It will take you the rest of your life to renew your mind and conform to the image of God. If your problems stem from a source other than those covered in these steps, you may need to seek professional help.

May the Lord grace you with His presence as you seek His face and help others experience the joy of their salvation.

—Neil T. Anderson

Prayer

Dear heavenly Father, we acknowledge Your presence in this room and in our lives. You are the only omniscient (all-knowing), omnipotent (all-powerful), and omnipresent (always present) God. We are dependent upon You, for apart from You we can do nothing. We stand in the truth that all authority in heaven and on earth has been given to the resurrected Christ, and because we are in Christ, we share that authority in order to make disciples and set captives free. We ask You to fill us with Your Holy Spirit and lead us into all truth. We pray for Your complete protection and ask for Your guidance. In Jesus' name, amen.

Declaration

In the name and authority of the Lord Jesus Christ, we command Satan and all evil spirits to release _____ (name) in order that _____ (name) can be free to know and choose to do the will of God. As children of God seated with Christ in the heavenlies, we agree that every enemy of the Lord Jesus Christ be bound to silence. We say to Satan and all your evil workers that you cannot inflict any pain or in any way prevent God's will from being accomplished in _____ (name) life.

Preparation

Before going through the Steps, review the events of your life to discern specific areas that might need to be addressed.

Family History

- ❏ Religious history of parents and grandparents
- ❏ Home life from childhood through high school
- ❏ History of physical or emotional illness in the family
- ❏ Adoption, foster care, guardians

Personal History

- ❏ Eating habits (bulimia, bingeing and purging, anorexia, compulsive eating)
- ❏ Addictions (drugs, alcohol)
- ❏ Prescription medications (what for?)
- ❏ Sleeping patterns and nightmares
- ❏ Rape or any other sexual, physical, emotional abuse
- ❏ Thought life (obsessive, blasphemous, condemning, distracting thoughts, poor concentration, fantasy)
- ❏ Mental interference during church, prayer or Bible study
- ❏ Emotional life (anger, anxiety, depression, bitterness, fears)
- ❏ Spiritual journey (salvation: when, how, and assurance)

Now you are ready to begin. The following are seven specific steps to process in order to experience freedom from your past. You will address the areas where Satan most commonly takes advantage of us and where strongholds have been built. Christ purchased your victory when He shed His blood for you on the cross. Realizing your freedom will be the result of what you choose to believe, confess, forgive, renounce and forsake. No one can do that for you. The battle for your mind can only be won as you personally choose truth.

As you go through these Steps to Freedom, remember that Satan will only be defeated if you confront him verbally. He cannot read your mind and is under no obligation to obey your thoughts. Only God has complete knowledge of your mind. As you process each step, it is important that you submit to God inwardly and resist the devil by reading aloud each prayer—verbally renouncing, forgiving, confessing, and so forth.

You are taking a fierce moral inventory and making a rock-solid commitment to truth. If your problems stem from a source other than those covered in these steps, you have nothing to lose by going through them. If you are sincere, the only thing that can happen is that you will get very right with God!

Step 1
Counterfeit vs. Real

The first Step to Freedom in Christ is to renounce your previous or current involvement with satanically inspired occult practices and false religions. You need to renounce any activity or group that denies Jesus Christ, offers guidance through any source other than the absolute authority of the written Word of God or requires secret initiations, ceremonies or covenants.

In order to help you assess your spiritual experiences, begin this step by asking God to reveal false guidance and counterfeit religious experiences.

> *Dear heavenly Father, I ask You to guard my heart and my mind and reveal to me any and all involvement I have had either knowingly or unknowingly with cultic or occult practices, false religions or false teachers. In Jesus' name, I pray. Amen.*

Using the Non-Christian Spiritual Experience Inventory on the following page, carefully check anything in which you were involved. This list is not exhaustive, but it will guide you in identifying non-Christian experiences. Add any additional involvement you have had. Even if you innocently participated in something or observed it, you should write it on your list to renounce, just in case you unknowingly gave Satan a foothold.

Non-Christian Spiritual Experience Inventory
Please check all those that apply.

- ❏ Astral-projection
- ❏ Ouija board
- ❏ Table or body lifting
- ❏ Dungeons and Dragons
- ❏ Speaking in trance
- ❏ Automatic writing
- ❏ Magic Eight Ball
- ❏ Telepathy
- ❏ Using spells or curses
- ❏ Séance
- ❏ Materialization
- ❏ Clairvoyance
- ❏ Spirit guides
- ❏ Fortune-telling
- ❏ Tarot cards
- ❏ Palm reading
- ❏ Astrology/horoscopes
- ❏ Rod/pendulum (dowsing)
- ❏ Self-hypnosis
- ❏ Mental manipulations or attempts to swap minds
- ❏ New Age medicine

- ❏ Black and white magic
- ❏ Blood pacts or self-mutilation
- ❏ Fetishism (objects of worship, crystals, good-luck charms)
- ❏ Incubi and succubi (sexual spirits)
- ❏ Other _____
  _____
- ❏ Christian Science
- ❏ The Way International
- ❏ Unification Church
- ❏ Mormonism
- ❏ Church of the Living Word
- ❏ Jehovah's Witnesses
- ❏ Children of God (Love)
- ❏ Swedenborgianism
- ❏ Unitarianism
- ❏ Masons
- ❏ New Age
- ❏ The Forum (EST)

- ❏ Spirit worship
- ❏ Other _____
  _____
- ❏ Buddhism
- ❏ Hare Krishna
- ❏ Bahaism
- ❏ Rosicrucianism
- ❏ Science of the Mind
- ❏ Science of Creative Intelligence
- ❏ Transcendental Meditation (TM)
- ❏ Hinduism
- ❏ Yoga
- ❏ Echkankar
- ❏ Roy Masters
- ❏ Silva Mind Control
- ❏ Father Divine
- ❏ Theosophical Society
- ❏ Islam
- ❏ Black Muslim
- ❏ Religion of martial arts
- ❏ Other _____
  _____

Now answer the following questions:

1. Have you ever been hypnotized, attended a New Age or parapsychology seminar or consulted a medium, spiritist or channeler? Explain.

    _____
    _____
    _____
    _____
    _____
    _____
    _____
    _____
    _____
    _____
    _____
    _____

2. Do you or have you ever had an imaginary friend or spirit guide offering you guidance or companionship? Explain.

    _____
    _____
    _____
    _____
    _____
    _____
    _____
    _____
    _____
    _____
    _____
    _____

3. Have you ever heard voices in your mind or had repeating and nagging thoughts condemning you or that were foreign to what you believe or feel, as if there were a dialogue going on in your head? Explain.

_____

_____

_____

_____

_____

_____

_____

_____

_____

_____

_____

4. What other spiritual experiences have you had that would be considered out of the ordinary?

_____

_____

_____

_____

_____

_____

_____

_____

_____

_____

_____

_____

5. Have you ever made a vow, covenant or pact with any individual or group other than God?

_____

_____

_____

_____

_____

_____

_____

_____

_____

6. Have you been involved in satanic ritual or satanic worship in any form? Explain.

_____

_____

_____

_____

_____

_____

_____

_____

_____

When you are confident that your list is complete, confess and renounce each involvement whether active or passive by praying aloud the following prayer, repeating it separately for each item on your list:

Lord, I confess that I have participated in _____, and I renounce _____. Thank You that in Christ I am forgiven.

If there has been any involvement in satanic ritual or heavy occult activity, you need to state aloud the following special renunciations that apply. Read across the page, renouncing the first item in the column of the Kingdom of Darkness and then affirming the first truth in the column of the Kingdom of Light. Continue down the page in this manner.

Kingdom of Darkness	Kingdom of Light
I renounce ever signing my name over to Satan or having had my name signed over to Satan.	I announce that my name is now written in the Lamb's Book of Life.
I renounce any ceremony where I might have been wed to Satan.	I announce that I am the bride of Christ.
I renounce any and all covenants that I made with Satan.	I announce that I am a partaker of the New Covenant with Christ.
I renounce all satanic assignments for my life, including duties, marriage and children.	I announce and commit myself to know and do only the will of God and accept only His guidance.
I renounce all spirit guides assigned to me.	I announce and accept only the leading of the Holy Spirit.
I renounce ever giving of my blood in the service of Satan.	I trust only in the shed blood of my Lord Jesus Christ.
I renounce ever eating of flesh or drinking of blood for satanic worship.	By faith I eat only the flesh and drink only the blood of Jesus in Holy Communion.
I renounce any and all guardians and satanist parents who were assigned to me.	I announce that God is my Father and the Holy Spirit is my Guardian by which I am sealed.
I renounce any baptism in blood or urine whereby I am identified with Satan.	I announce that I have been baptized into Christ Jesus and my identity is now in Christ.
I renounce any and all sacrifices that were made on my behalf by which Satan may claim ownership of me.	I announce that only the sacrifice of Christ has any hold on me. I belong to Him. I have been purchased by the blood of the Lamb.

All satanic rituals, covenants and assignments must be specifically renounced as the Lord allows you to recall them. Some who have been subjected to satanic ritual abuse may have developed multiple personalities in order to survive. Nevertheless, continue through the Steps to Freedom in order to resolve all that you consciously can. It is important that you resolve the demonic strongholds first. Every personality must resolve his/her issues and agree to come together in Christ. You may need someone who understands spiritual conflict to help you maintain control and not be deceived into false memories. Only Jesus can bind up the brokenhearted, set captives free and make us whole.

Step 2
Deception vs. Truth

Truth is the revelation of God's Word, but we need to acknowledge the truth in the inner self (see Psalm 51:6). When David lived a lie, he suffered greatly. When he finally found freedom by acknowledging the truth, he wrote, "Blessed is the man . . . in whose spirit is no deceit" (Psalm 32:2). We are to lay aside falsehood and speak the truth in love (see Ephesians 4:15,25). A mentally healthy person is one who is in touch with reality and relatively free of anxiety. Both qualities should characterize the Christian who renounces deception and embraces the truth.

Begin this critical step by expressing aloud the following prayer. Don't let the enemy accuse you with thoughts such as: *This isn't going to work* or *I wish I could believe this, but I can't* or any other lies in opposition to what you are proclaiming. Even if you have difficulty doing so, you need to pray the prayer and read the Doctrinal Affirmation.

> *Dear heavenly Father, I know that You desire truth in the inner self and that facing this truth is the way of liberation (see John 8:32). I acknowledge that I have been deceived by the father of*

lies (see John 8:44) and that I have deceived myself (see 1 John 1:8). I pray in the name of the Lord Jesus Christ that You, heavenly Father, will rebuke all deceiving spirits by virtue of the shed blood and resurrection of the Lord Jesus Christ. By faith I have received You into my life and I am now seated with Christ in the heavenlies [see Ephesians 2:6]. I acknowledge that I have the responsibility and authority to resist the devil, and when I do, he will flee from me. I now ask the Holy Spirit to guide me into all truth [see John 16:13]. I ask You to "search me, O God, and know my heart; try me and know my anxious thoughts; and see if there be any hurtful way in me, and lead me in the everlasting way" [Psalm 139:23,24, NASB]. In Jesus' name, I pray. Amen.

You may want to pause at this point to consider some of Satan's deceptive schemes. In addition to false teachers, false prophets and deceiving spirits, you can deceive yourself. Now that you are alive in Christ and forgiven, you never have to live a lie or defend yourself. Christ is your defense. How have you deceived or attempted to defend yourself according to the following? Please check any of the following that apply to you:

Self-Deception
❑ Hearing God's Word but not doing it (see James 1:22; 4:17)
❑ Saying you have no sin (see 1 John 1:8)
❑ Thinking that you are something when you aren't (see Galatians 6:3)
❑ Thinking you are wise in your own eyes (see 1 Corinthians 3:18-19)
❑ Thinking you will not reap what you sow (see Galatians 6:7)
❑ Thinking the unrighteous will inherit the kingdom (see 1 Corinthians 6:9)
❑ Thinking you can associate with bad company and not be corrupted (see 1 Corinthians 15:33)

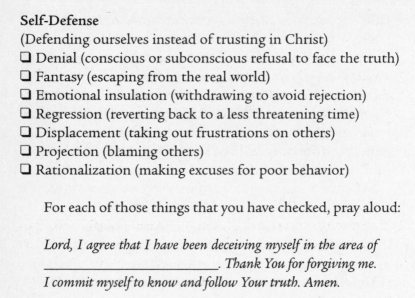

Self-Defense
(Defending ourselves instead of trusting in Christ)
❑ Denial (conscious or subconscious refusal to face the truth)
❑ Fantasy (escaping from the real world)
❑ Emotional insulation (withdrawing to avoid rejection)
❑ Regression (reverting back to a less threatening time)
❑ Displacement (taking out frustrations on others)
❑ Projection (blaming others)
❑ Rationalization (making excuses for poor behavior)

For each of those things that you have checked, pray aloud:

Lord, I agree that I have been deceiving myself in the area of
_____. *Thank You for forgiving me.*
I commit myself to know and follow Your truth. Amen.

Choosing the truth may be difficult if you have been living a lie (being deceived) for many years. You may need to seek professional help to weed out the defense mechanisms you have depended upon to survive. The Christian needs only one defense: Jesus. Knowing that you are forgiven and accepted as God's child is what sets you free to face reality and declare your dependence on Him.

Faith is the biblical response to the truth and believing the truth is a choice. When someone says, "I want to believe God, but I just can't," they are being deceived. Of course you can believe God. Faith is something you decide to do, not something you feel like doing. Believing the truth doesn't make it true. It's true; therefore, we believe it. The New Age movement has been distorting the truth by saying we create reality through what we believe. We can't create reality with our minds; we face reality. It is what or who you believe in that counts. Everybody believes in something, and everybody walks by faith according to what he or she believes. But if what you believe isn't true, then how you live (walk by faith) won't be right.

Historically, the Church has found great value in publicly declaring its beliefs. The Apostles' Creed and the Nicene Creed have been recited for centuries. Read aloud the following affirmation of faith, and do so again as often as necessary to renew your mind. Experiencing difficulty in reading this affirmation may indicate where you are being deceived and under attack. Boldly affirm your commitment to biblical truth.

Doctrinal Affirmation

I recognize that there is only one true and living God (see Exodus 20:2-3) who exists as the Father, Son and Holy Spirit and that He is worthy of all honor, praise and glory as the Creator, Sustainer and Beginning and End of all things (see Revelation 4:11; 5:9-10; 22:13; Isaiah 43:1,7,21).

I recognize Jesus Christ as the Messiah, the Word who became flesh and dwelt among us (see John 1:1,14). I believe that He came to destroy the works of Satan (see 1 John 3:8), that He disarmed the rulers and authorities and made a public display of them, having triumphed over them (see Colossians 2:15).

I believe that God has proven His love for me because when I was still a sinner, Christ died for me (see Romans 5:8). I believe that He delivered me from the domain of darkness and transferred me to His kingdom, and in Him I have redemption— the forgiveness of sins (see Colossians 1:13-14).

I believe that I am now a child of God (see 1 John 3:1-3) and that I am seated with Christ in the heavenlies (see Ephesians 2:6). I believe that I was saved by the grace of God through faith, that it was a gift, and not the result of any works on my part (see Ephesians 2:8-9).

I choose to be strong in the Lord and in the strength of His might (see Ephesians 6:10). I put no confidence in the flesh (see Philippians 3:3) for the weapons of warfare are not of the flesh (see 2 Corinthians 10:4). I put on the whole armor of God (see Ephesians 6:10-20), and I resolve to stand firm in my faith and resist the evil one.

I believe that apart from Christ I can do nothing (see John 15:5), so I declare myself dependent on Him. I choose to abide in Christ in order to bear much fruit and glorify the Lord (see John 15:8). I announce to Satan that Jesus is my Lord (see 1 Corinthians 12:3), and I reject any counterfeit gifts or works of Satan in my life.

I believe that the truth will set me free (see John 8:32) and that walking in the light is the only path of fellowship (see 1 John 1:7). Therefore, I stand against Satan's deception by taking every thought captive in obedience to Christ (see 2 Corinthians 10:5). I declare that the Bible is the only authoritative standard (see 2 Timothy 3:15-16). I choose to speak the truth in love (see Ephesians 4:15).

I choose to present my body as an instrument of righteousness, a living and holy sacrifice, and I renew my mind by the living Word of God in order that I may prove that the will of God is good, acceptable and perfect (see Romans 6:13; 12:1-2). I put off the old self with its evil practices and put on the new self (see Colossians 3:9-10), and I declare myself to be a new creature in Christ (see 2 Corinthians 5:17).

I trust my heavenly Father to fill me with His Holy Spirit (see Ephesians 5:18), to lead me into all truth (see John 16:13), and to empower my life that I may live above sin and not carry out the desires of the flesh (see Galatians 5:16). I crucify the flesh (see Galatians 5:24) and choose to walk by the Spirit.

I renounce all selfish goals and choose the ultimate goal of love (see 1 Timothy 1:5). I choose to obey the two greatest commandments: to love the Lord my God with all my heart, soul and mind, and to love my neighbor as myself (see Matthew 22:37-39).

I believe that Jesus has all authority in heaven and on earth (see Matthew 28:18) and that He is the Head over all rule and authority (see Colossians 2:10). I believe that Satan and his demons are subject to me in Christ since I am a member of Christ's Body (see Ephesians 1:19-23). Therefore, I obey the command to submit to God and to resist the devil (see James 4:7), and I command Satan in the name of Christ to leave my presence.

Step 3
Bitterness vs. Forgiveness

We need to forgive others in order to be free from our pasts and to prevent Satan from taking advantage of us (see 2 Corinthians 2:10-11). We are to be merciful just as our heavenly Father is merciful (see Luke 6:36). We are to forgive as we have been forgiven (see Ephesians 4:31-32). Ask God to bring to mind the names of those people you need to forgive by expressing the following prayer aloud:

> *Dear heavenly Father, I thank You for the riches of Your kindness, forbearance and patience, knowing that Your kindness has led me to repentance [see Romans 2:4]. I confess that I have not extended that same patience and kindness toward others who have offended me, but instead I have harbored bitterness and resentment. I pray that during this time of self-examination You would bring to my mind those people that I need to forgive in order that I may do so [see Matthew 18:35]. I ask this in the precious name of Jesus. Amen.*

As names come to mind, list them on a separate sheet of paper. At the end of your list, write "myself." Forgiving yourself is accepting God's cleansing and forgiveness. Also, write "thoughts against God." Thoughts raised up against the knowledge of God will usually result in angry feelings toward Him. Technically, we don't forgive God because He cannot commit any sin of commission or omission. But we do need to specifically renounce false expectations and thoughts about God and agree to release any anger we have toward Him.

Before you pray to forgive these people, stop and consider what forgiveness is, what it is not, what decision you will be making and what the consequences will be. In the following explanation, the main points are in bold print:

Forgiveness is not forgetting. People who try to forget find they cannot. God says He will remember our sins no more (see Hebrews 10:17), but God, being omniscient, cannot forget. Remember our sins no more means that God will never use the past against us (see Psalm 103:12). Forgetting may be the result of forgiveness, but it is never the means of forgiveness. When we bring up the past against others, we are saying we haven't forgiven them.

Forgiveness is a choice, a crisis of the will. Since God requires us to forgive, it is something we can do. However, forgiveness is difficult for us because it pulls against our concept of justice. We want revenge for offenses suffered. However, we are told never to take our own revenge (see Romans 12:19). You say, "Why should I let them off the hook?" That is precisely the problem. You are still hooked to them, still bound by your past. **You will let them off your hook, but they are never off God's.** He will deal with them fairly—something we cannot do.

You say, "You don't understand how much this person hurt me!" But don't you see, they are still hurting you! How do you stop the pain? **You don't forgive someone for their sake; you do it for your own sake so that you can be free. Your need to forgive isn't an issue between you and the offender; it's between you and God.**

Forgiveness is agreeing to live with the consequences of another person's sin. Forgiveness is costly. You pay the price of the evil you forgive. You're going to live with those consequences whether you want to or not; your only choice is whether you will do so in the bitterness of unforgiveness or the freedom of forgiveness. Jesus took the consequences of your sin upon Himself. All true forgiveness is substitutionary because no one really forgives without bearing the consequences of the other person's sin. God the Father "made Him who knew no sin to be sin on our behalf, that we might become the righteousness of God in Him" (2 Corinthians 5:21). Where is the justice? It's the cross that makes forgiveness legally and morally right: "For the death that He died, He died to sin, once for all" (Romans 6:10).

Decide that you will bear the burdens of their offenses by not using that information against them in the future. This doesn't mean that you tolerate sin. You must set up scriptural boundaries to prevent future abuse. Some may be required to testify for the sake of justice but not for the purpose of seeking revenge from a bitter heart.

How do you forgive from your heart? You acknowledge the hurt and the hate. If your forgiveness doesn't visit the emotional core of your life, it will be incomplete. Many feel the pain of interpersonal offenses, but they won't or don't know how to acknowledge it. Let God bring the pain to the surface so that He can deal with it. This is where the healing takes place.

Don't wait to forgive until you feel like forgiving; you will never get there. Feelings take time to heal after the choice to forgive is made and Satan has lost his place (see Ephesians 4:26-27). **Freedom is what will be gained, not a feeling.**

As you pray, God may bring to mind offending people and experiences you have totally forgotten. Let Him do it even if it is painful. Remember, you are doing this for your sake. God wants you to be free. Don't rationalize or explain the offender's behavior. Forgiveness is dealing with your pain and leaving the other person to God. Positive feelings will follow in time; freeing you from the past is the critical issue right now.

Don't say, "Lord, please help me to forgive," because He is already helping you. Don't say, "Lord, I want to forgive," because you are bypassing the hard-core choice to forgive that is your responsibility. Focus on each individual until you are sure you have dealt with all the remembered pain—what they did, how they hurt you, how they made you feel: rejected, unloved, unworthy, dirty, and so forth.

You are now ready to forgive the people on your list so that you can be free in Christ, with those people no longer having any control over you. For each person on your list, pray the following prayer aloud:

Lord, I forgive _____ (name the person) for _____ (verbally share every hurt and pain the Lord brings to your mind and how it made you feel).

After you have forgiven every person for every painful memory, then finish this step by praying:

Lord, I release all these people to You, and I release my right to seek revenge. I choose not to hold on to my bitterness and anger, and I ask You to heal my damaged emotions. In Jesus' name, I pray. Amen.

Step 4
Rebellion vs. Submission

We live in rebellious times. Many believe it is their right to sit in judgment of those in authority over them. Rebelling against God and His authority gives Satan an opportunity to attack. As our commanding General, the Lord tells us to get into ranks and follow Him; He will not lead us into temptation, but will deliver us from evil (see Matthew 6:13).

We have two biblical responsibilities regarding authority figures: Pray for them and submit to them. The only time God permits us to disobey earthly leaders is when they require us to do something morally wrong before God or attempt to rule outside the realm of their authority. Pray the following prayer:

Dear heavenly Father, You have said that rebellion is like the sin of witchcraft and insubordination is like iniquity and idolatry [see 1 Samuel 15:23]. I know that in action and attitude I have sinned against You with a rebellious heart. Thank You for forgiving my rebellion, and I pray that by the shed blood of the Lord Jesus Christ all ground gained by evil spirits because of my rebelliousness will be canceled. I pray that You will shed light on all my ways that I may know the full extent of my rebelliousness. I now choose to adopt a submissive spirit and a servant's heart. In the name of Christ Jesus, my Lord, amen.

Being under authority is an act of faith. You are trusting God to work through His established lines of authority. There are times when employers, parents and spouses are violating the laws of civil government that are ordained by God to protect innocent people against abuse. In these cases, you need to appeal to the state for your protection. In many states, the law requires such abuse to be reported.

In difficult cases, such as continuing abuse at home, further counseling help may be needed. And, in some cases, when earthly authorities have abused their position and are requiring disobedience to God or a compromise in your commitment to Him, you need to obey God, not man. We are all admonished to submit to one another as equals in Christ (see Ephesians 5:21). However, there are specific lines of authority in Scripture for the purpose of accomplishing common goals:

- Civil government (see Romans 13:1-7; 1 Timothy 2:1-4; 1 Peter 2:13-17)
- Parents (see Ephesians 6:1-3)
- Husbands (see 1 Peter 3:1-4) or wives (see Ephesians 5:21; 1 Peter 3:7)
- Employers (see 1 Peter 2:18-23)
- Church leaders (see Hebrews 13:17)
- God (see Daniel 9:5,9)

Examine each area and confess those times you have not been submissive by praying:

Lord, I agree I have been rebellious toward _____.
I choose to be submissive and obedient to Your Word. In Jesus'
name, amen.

Step 5
Pride vs. Humility

Pride is a killer. Pride says, "I can do it! I can get myself out of this mess without God or anyone else's help." Oh no, we can't!

We absolutely need God, and we desperately need each other. Paul wrote, "For it is . . . we who worship by the Spirit of God, who glory in Christ Jesus, and who put no confidence in the flesh" (Philippians 3:3). Humility is confidence properly placed. We are to be "strong in the Lord and in his mighty power" (Ephesians 6:10). James 4:6-10 and 1 Peter 5:1-10 reveal that spiritual conflict follows pride. Use the following prayer to express your commitment to live humbly before God:

Dear heavenly Father, You have said that pride goes before destruction and an arrogant spirit before stumbling [see Proverbs 16:18]. I confess that I have lived independently and have not denied myself, picked up my cross daily and followed You [see Matthew 16:24]. In so doing, I have given ground to the enemy in my life. I have believed that I could be successful and live victoriously by my own strength and resources. I now confess that I have sinned against You by placing my will before Yours and by centering my life around myself instead of You. I now renounce the self-life and by so doing cancel all the ground that has been gained in my members by the enemies of the Lord Jesus Christ. I pray that You will guide me so that I will do nothing from selfishness or empty conceit, but with humility of mind I will regard others as more important than myself [see Philippians 2:3]. Enable me through love to serve others and in honor prefer others [see Romans 12:10]. I ask this in the name of Christ Jesus, my Lord. Amen.

Having made that commitment, now allow God to show you any specific areas of your life where you have been prideful, such as the following:

- ❑ Having a stronger desire to do my will than God's will
- ❑ Being more dependent upon my strengths and resources than God's

- ❏ Too often believing that my ideas and opinions are better than others'
- ❏ Being more concerned about controlling others than developing self-control
- ❏ Sometimes considering myself more important than other people
- ❏ Having a tendency to think that I have no needs
- ❏ Finding it difficult to admit that I was wrong
- ❏ Having a tendency to be more of a people-pleaser than a God-pleaser
- ❏ Being overly concerned about getting the credit I deserve
- ❏ Being driven to obtain the recognition that comes from degrees, titles and positions
- ❏ Often thinking I am more humble than others
- ❏ These other ways:

_____

_____

_____

_____

_____

_____

_____

For each of these that has been true in your life, pray aloud:

Lord, I agree I have been prideful by _____.
I choose to humble myself and place all my confidence in You.
Amen.

Step 6
Bondage vs. Freedom

The next step to freedom deals with habitual sin. People who have been caught in the trap of sin-confess-sin-confess may need to follow the instructions of James 5:16: "Confess your sins to each other and pray for each other so that you may be healed. The prayer of a righteous man is powerful and effective." Seek out a righteous person who will hold you up in prayer and to whom you can be accountable. Others may only need the assurance of 1 John 1:9: "If we confess our sins, He is faithful and righteous to forgive us our sins and to cleanse us from all unrighteousness." Confession is not saying, "I'm sorry"; it is saying, "I did it." Whether you need the help of others or just the accountability to God, pray the following prayer:

Dear heavenly Father, You have told us to put on the Lord Jesus Christ and make no provision for the flesh in regard to its lust [see Romans 13:14, NASB]. I acknowledge that I have given in to fleshly lusts that wage war against my soul [see 1 Peter 2:11]. I thank You that in Christ my sins are forgiven, but I have transgressed Your holy law and given the enemy an opportunity to wage war in my physical body [see Romans 6:12-13; Ephesians 4:27; James 4:1; 1 Peter 5:8]. I come before Your presence to acknowledge these sins and to seek Your cleansing [see 1 John 1:9], that I may be freed from the bondage of sin. I now ask You to reveal to my mind the ways that I have transgressed Your moral law and grieved the Holy Spirit. In Jesus' precious name, I pray. Amen.

The deeds of the flesh are numerous. Many of the following issues are from Galatians 5:19-21. Check those that apply to you and any others you have struggled with that the Lord has brought to your mind. Then confess each one with the concluding prayer.

Note: Sexual sins, eating disorders, substance abuse, abortion, suicidal tendencies, perfectionism and fear will be dealt with later in this Step.

❏ Stealing	❏ Cheating	❏ Other:
❏ Lying	❏ Gossiping	_____
❏ Fighting	❏ Controlling	_____
❏ Jealousy	❏ Procrastinating	_____
❏ Envying	❏ Swearing	_____
❏ Outbursts of anger	❏ Greediness	_____
❏ Complaining	❏ Laziness	_____
❏ Criticizing	❏ Divisiveness	_____
❏ Lusting	❏ Gambling	_____

Dear heavenly Father, I thank You that my sins are forgiven in Christ, but I have walked by the flesh and therefore sinned by _____. Thank You for cleansing me of all unrighteousness. I ask that You would enable me to walk by the Spirit and not carry out the desires of the flesh. In Jesus' name, I pray. Amen.

It is our responsibility not to allow sin to reign in our mortal bodies by not using our bodies as instruments of unrighteousness (see Romans 6:12-13). If you are struggling or have struggled with sexual sins (pornography, masturbation, sexual promiscuity, etc.) or are experiencing sexual difficulty in your marriage, pray as follows:

Lord, I ask You to reveal to my mind every sexual use of my body as an instrument of unrighteousness. In Jesus' precious name, I pray. Amen.

As the Lord brings to your mind every sexual misuse of your body, whether it was done to you—rape, incest or other sexual abuse—or willingly by you, renounce every occasion:

Lord, I renounce _____(name the specific misuse of your body) with _____(name the person) and ask You to break that bond.

Now commit your body to the Lord by praying:

Lord, I renounce all these uses of my body as an instrument of unrighteousness and by so doing ask You to break all bondages Satan has brought into my life through that involvement. I confess my participation. I now present my body to You as a living sacrifice, holy and acceptable unto You, and I reserve the sexual use of my body only for marriage. I renounce the lie of Satan that my body is not clean, that it is dirty or in any way unacceptable as a result of my past sexual experiences. Lord, I thank You that You have totally cleansed and forgiven me, that You love and accept me unconditionally. Therefore, I can accept myself. And I choose to do so, to accept myself and my body as cleansed. In Jesus' name, amen.

Special Prayers for Specific Problems

Homosexuality

Lord, I renounce the lie that You have created me or anyone else to be homosexual, and I affirm that You clearly forbid homosexual behavior. I accept myself as a child of God and declare that You created me a man (woman). I renounce any bondages of Satan that have perverted my relationships with others. I announce that I am free to relate to the opposite sex in the way that You intended. In Jesus' name, amen.

Abortion

Lord, I confess that I did not assume stewardship of the life You entrusted to me. I choose to accept Your forgiveness, and I now

*commit that child to You for Your care in eternity. In Jesus'
name, amen.*

Suicidal Tendencies

*Lord, I renounce suicidal thoughts and any attempts I have
made to take my own life or in any way injure myself. I renounce the lie that life is hopeless and that I can find peace and
freedom by taking my own life. Satan is a thief and he comes
to steal, kill and destroy. I choose to be a good steward of the
physical life that You have entrusted to me. In Jesus' name,
I pray. Amen.*

Eating Disorders or Self-Mutilation

*Lord, I renounce the lie that my value as a person is dependent
upon my physical beauty, my weight or size. I renounce cutting
myself, vomiting, using laxatives or starving myself as a means
of cleansing myself of evil or altering my appearance. I announce that only the blood of the Lord Jesus Christ cleanses me
from sin. I accept the reality that there may be sin present in me
due to the lies I have believed and the wrongful use of my body,
but I renounce the lie that I am evil or that any part of my body
is evil. My body is the temple of the Holy Spirit and I belong to
You, Lord. I receive Your love and acceptance of me. In Jesus'
name, amen.*

Substance Abuse

*Lord, I confess that I have misused substances (alcohol, tobacco,
food, prescription or street drugs) for the purpose of pleasure, to
escape reality or to cope with difficult situations—resulting in
the abuse of my body, the harmful programming of my mind
and the quenching of the Holy Spirit. I ask Your forgiveness.*

I renounce any satanic connection or influence in my life through my misuse of chemicals or food. I cast my anxiety onto Christ who loves me, and I commit myself to no longer yield to substance abuse, but to the Holy Spirit. I ask You, heavenly Father, to fill me with Your Holy Spirit. In Jesus' name, amen.

Drivenness and Perfectionism

Lord, I renounce the lie that my self-worth is dependent upon my ability to perform. I announce the truth that my identity and sense of worth are found in who I am as Your child. I renounce seeking the approval and acceptance of other people, and I choose to believe that I am already approved and accepted in Christ because of His death and resurrection for me. I choose to believe the truth that I have been saved, not by deeds done in righteousness, but according to Your mercy. I choose to believe that I am no longer under the curse of the law because Christ became a curse for me. I receive the free gift of life in Christ and choose to abide in Him. I renounce striving for perfection by living under the law. By Your grace, heavenly Father, I choose from this day forward to walk by faith according to what You have said is true by the power of Your Holy Spirit. In Jesus' name, amen.

Plaguing Fears

Dear heavenly Father, I acknowledge You as the only legitimate fear object in my life. You are the only omnipresent (always present) and omniscient (all-knowing) God and the only means by which all other fears can be expelled. You are my sanctuary. You have not given me a spirit of timidity, but of power and love and discipline. I confess that I have allowed the fear of man and the fear of death to exercise control over my life instead of trusting in You. I now renounce all other fear objects and worship You only. I pray that You would fill me with Your Holy Spirit that I may live my life and speak Your Word with boldness. In Jesus' name, I pray. Amen.

After you have confessed all known sin, pray:

Dear heavenly Father, I now confess these sins to You and claim my forgiveness and cleansing through the blood of the Lord Jesus Christ. I cancel all ground that evil spirits have gained through my willful involvement in sin. I ask this in the wonderful name of my Lord and Savior, Jesus Christ. Amen.

Step 7
Acquiescence vs. Renunciation

Acquiescence is passively giving in or agreeing without consent. The last step to freedom is to renounce the sins of your ancestors and any curses that may have been placed on you. In giving the Ten Commandments, God said, "You shall not make for yourself an idol, or any likeness of what is in heaven above or on the earth beneath or in the water under the earth. You shall not worship them or serve them; for I, the LORD your God, am a jealous God, visiting the iniquity of the fathers on the children, on the third and the fourth generations of those who hate Me" (Exodus 20:4-5).

Familiar spirits can be passed on from one generation to the next if not renounced and if your new spiritual heritage in Christ is not proclaimed. You are not guilty for the sin of any ancestor, but because of their sin, Satan may have gained access to your family. This is not to deny that many problems are transmitted genetically or acquired from an immoral atmosphere. All three conditions can predispose an individual to a particular sin. In addition, deceived people may try to curse you, or satanic groups may try to target you. You have all the authority and protection you need in Christ to stand against such curses and assignments.

Ask the Lord to reveal to your mind the sins and iniquities of your ancestors by praying the following prayer:

Dear heavenly Father, I thank You that I am a new creation in Christ. I desire to obey Your command to honor my mother and my father, but I also acknowledge that my physical heritage has not been perfect. I ask You to reveal to my mind the sins and iniquities of my ancestors in order to confess, renounce and forsake them. In Jesus' name, I pray. Amen.

Now claim your position and protection in Christ by making the following declaration verbally, and then by humbling yourself before God in prayer.

Declaration

I here and now reject and disown all the sins and iniquities of my ancestors, including _____ _____ (name them). As one who has been delivered from the power of darkness and translated into the kingdom of God's dear Son, I cancel out all demonic working that has been passed on to me from my ancestors. As one who has been crucified and raised with Jesus Christ and who sits with Him in heavenly places, I renounce all satanic assignments that are directed toward me and my ministry, and I cancel every curse that Satan and his workers have put on me. I announce to Satan and all his forces that Christ became a curse for me (see Galatians 3:13) when He died for my sins on the cross. I reject any and every way in which Satan may claim ownership of me. I belong to the Lord Jesus Christ who purchased me with His own blood.

I reject all other blood sacrifices whereby Satan may claim ownership of me. I declare myself to be eternally and completely signed over and committed to the Lord Jesus Christ. By the authority I have in Jesus Christ, I now command every spiritual enemy of the Lord Jesus Christ to leave my presence. I commit myself to my heavenly Father to do His will from this day forward.

Prayer

Dear heavenly Father, I come to You as Your child purchased by the blood of the Lord Jesus Christ. You are the Lord of the universe and the Lord of my life. I submit my body to You as an instrument of righteousness, a living sacrifice, that I may glorify You in my body. I now ask You to fill me with Your Holy Spirit. I commit myself to the renewing of my mind in order to prove that Your will is good, perfect and acceptable for me. All this I do in the name and authority of the Lord Jesus Christ. Amen.

Once you have secured your freedom by going through these seven steps, you may find demonic influences attempting reentry, days or even months later. One person shared that she heard a spirit say to her mind, "I'm back," two days after she had been set free. "No, you're not!" she proclaimed aloud. The attack ceased immediately. One victory does not constitute winning the war. Freedom must be maintained. After completing these steps, one jubilant lady asked, "Will I always be like this?" I told her that she would stay free as long as she remained in right relationship with God. "Even if you slip and fall," I encouraged, "you know how to get right with God again."

One victim of incredible atrocities shared this illustration: "It's like being forced to play a game with an ugly stranger in my own home. I kept losing and wanted to quit, but the ugly stranger wouldn't let me. Finally I called the police (a higher authority), and they came and escorted the stranger out. He knocked on the door trying to regain entry, but this time I recognized his voice and didn't let him in."

What a beautiful illustration of gaining freedom in Christ. We call upon Jesus, the ultimate authority, and He escorts the enemy out of our lives. Know the truth, stand firm and resist the evil one. Seek out good Christian fellowship, and commit yourself to regular times of Bible study and prayer. God loves you and will never leave or forsake you.

Aftercare

Freedom must be maintained. You have won a very important battle in an ongoing war. Freedom is yours as long as you keep choosing truth and standing firm in the strength of the Lord. If new memories should surface or if you become aware of lies that you have believed or other non-Christian experiences you have had, renounce them and choose the truth. Some have found it helpful to go through the steps again. As you do, read the instructions carefully.

For your encouragement and further study, read *Victory Over the Darkness* (or the youth version *Stomping Out the Darkness*), *The Bondage Breaker* (adult or youth version) and *Released from Bondage*. If you are a parent, read *Spiritual Protection for Your Children*. *Walking in the Light* was written to help people understand God's guidance and discern counterfeit guidance. Also, to maintain your freedom, we suggest the following:

1. Seek legitimate Christian fellowship where you can walk in the light and speak the truth in love.

2. Study your Bible daily. Memorize key verses.

3. Take every thought captive to the obedience of Christ. Assume responsibility for your thought life, reject the

lie, choose the truth and stand firm in your position in Christ.

4. Don't drift away! It is very easy to get lazy in your thoughts and revert back to old habits or patterns of thinking. Share your struggles openly with a trusted friend. You need at least one friend who will stand with you.

5. Don't expect another person to fight your battle for you. Others can help, but they can't think, pray, read the Bible or choose the truth for you.

6. Continue to seek your identity and sense of worth in Christ. Read *Living Free in Christ* and the devotional *Daily in Christ*. Renew your mind with the truth that your acceptance, security and significance are in Christ by saturating your mind with the following truths. Read the entire list of who you are "In Christ" and the Doctrinal Affirmation (in Step 2) aloud morning and evening over the next several weeks (and look up the verses referenced).

7. Commit yourself to daily prayer. You can pray these suggested prayers often and with confidence:

Daily Prayer

Dear heavenly Father, I honor You as my sovereign Lord. I acknowledge that You are always present with me. You are the only all-powerful and wise God. You are kind and loving in all Your ways. I love You and thank You that I am united with Christ and spiritually alive in Him. I choose not to love the world, and I crucify the flesh and all its passions.

I thank You for the life that I now have in Christ, and I ask You to fill me with Your Holy Spirit, that I may live my life free from sin. I declare my dependence upon You, and I take my stand against Satan and all his lying ways. I choose to believe the truth and I refuse to be discouraged. You are the God of all hope, and I am confident that You will meet my needs as I seek to live according to Your Word. I express with confidence that I can live a responsible life through Christ who strengthens me.

I now take my stand against Satan and command him and all his evil spirits to depart from me. I put on the whole armor of God. I submit my body as a living sacrifice and renew my mind by the living Word of God in order that I may prove that the will of God is good, acceptable and perfect. I pray these things in the precious name of my Lord and Savior, Jesus Christ. Amen.

Bedtime Prayer

Thank You, Lord, that You have brought me into Your family and have blessed me with every spiritual blessing in the heavenly realms in Christ. Thank You for providing this time of renewal through sleep. I accept it as part of Your perfect plan for Your children, and I trust You to guard my mind and my body during my sleep. As I have meditated on You and Your truth during this day, I choose to let these thoughts continue in my mind while I am asleep. I commit myself to You for Your protection from every attempt of Satan or his emissaries to attack me during sleep. I commit myself to You as my Rock, my Fortress and my Resting Place. I pray in the strong name of the Lord Jesus Christ. Amen.

Cleansing Home/Apartment

After removing all articles of false worship from home/apartment, pray aloud in every room if necessary:

Heavenly Father, We/I acknowledge that You are Lord of heaven and earth. In Your sovereign power and love, You have given us/me all things richly to enjoy. Thank You for this place to live. We/I claim this home for our/my family as a place of spiritual safety and protection from all the attacks of the enemy. As children of God seated with Christ in the heavenly realm, we/I command every evil spirit claiming ground in the structures and furnishings of this place, based on the activities of previous occupants, to leave and never return. We/I renounce all curses and spells utilized against this place. We/I ask You, heavenly Father, to post guardian angels around this home (apartment, condo, room, etc.) to guard it from attempts of the enemy to enter and disturb Your purposes for us/me. We/I thank You, Lord, for doing this, and pray in the name of the Lord Jesus Christ. Amen.

Living in a Non-Christian Environment

After removing all articles of false worship from your room, pray aloud in the space allotted to you:

Thank You, heavenly Father, for my place to live and be renewed by sleep. I ask You to set aside my room (portion of my room) as a place of spiritual safety for me. I renounce any allegiance given to false gods or spirits by other occupants, and I renounce any claim to this room (space) by Satan based on activities of past occupants or me. On the basis of my position as a child of God and a joint-heir with Christ who has all authority in heaven and on earth, I command all evil spirits to leave this place and never to return. I ask You, heavenly Father, to appoint guardian angels to protect me while I live here. I pray this in the name of the Lord Jesus Christ. Amen.

In Christ

I Am Accepted

John 1:12	I am God's child.
John 15:15	I am Christ's friend.
Romans 5:1	I have been justified.
1 Corinthians 6:17	I am united with the Lord, and I am one spirit with Him.
1 Corinthians 6:20	I have been bought with a price. I belong to God.
1 Corinthians 12:27	I am a member of Christ's Body.
Ephesians 1:1	I am a saint.
Ephesians 1:5	I have been adopted as God's child.
Ephesians 2:18	I have direct access to God through the Holy Spirit.
Colossians 1:14	I have been redeemed and forgiven of all my sins.
Colossians 2:10	I am complete in Christ.

I Am Secure

Romans 8:1-2	I am free from condemnation.
Romans 8:28	I am assured that all things work together for good.
Romans 8:31-34	I am free from any condemning charges against me.
Romans 8:35-39	I cannot be separated from the love of God.
2 Corinthians 1:21-22	I have been established, anointed and sealed by God.
Colossians 3:3	I am hidden with Christ in God.
Philippians 1:6	I am confident that the good work God has begun in me will be perfected.
Philippians 3:20	I am a citizen of heaven.
2 Timothy 1:7	I have not been given a spirit of fear, but of power, love and a sound mind.
Hebrews 4:16	I can find grace and mercy to help in time of need.
1 John 5:18	I am born of God and the evil one cannot touch me.

I Am Significant

Matthew 5:13-14	I am the salt and light of the earth.
John 15:1,5	I am a branch of the true vine, a channel of His life.
John 15:16	I have been chosen and appointed to bear fruit.
Acts 1:8	I am a personal witness of Christ.
1 Corinthians 3:16	I am God's temple.
2 Corinthians 5:17-21	I am a minister of reconciliation for God.
2 Corinthians 6:1	I am God's coworker (see 1 Corinthians 3:9).
Ephesians 2:6	I am seated with Christ in the heavenly realm.
Ephesians 2:10	I am God's workmanship.
Ephesians 3:12	I may approach God with freedom and confidence.
Philippians 4:13	I can do all things through Christ who strengthens me.

Books and Resources by
Dr. Neil T. Anderson

About Dr. Neil T. Anderson

Dr. Neil T. Anderson was formerly the chairman of the Practical Theology Department at Talbot School of Theology. In 1989, he founded Freedom in Christ Ministries, which now has staff and offices in various countries around the world. He is currently on the Freedom in Christ Ministries International Board, which oversees this global ministry. For more information about Dr. Anderson and his ministry, visit his website at www.ficminternational.org.

Core Message and Materials

Victory Over the Darkness with study guide, audiobook and DVD (Regal Books, 2000). With over 1,000,000 copies in print, this core book explains who you are in Christ, how to walk by faith in the power of the Holy Spirit, how to be transformed by the renewing of your mind, how to experience emotional freedom, and how to relate to one another in Christ.

The Bondage Breaker with study guide, audiobook (Harvest House Publishers, 2000) and DVD (Regal Books, 2006). With over 1,000,000 copies in print, this book explains spiritual warfare, what our protection is, ways that we are vulnerable, and how we can live a liberated life in Christ.

Discipleship Counseling with DVD (Regal Books, 2003). This book combines the concepts of discipleship and counseling and teaches the practical integration of theology and psychology for helping Christians resolve their personal and spiritual conflicts through repentance and faith in God.

Steps to Freedom in Christ and interactive videocassette (Regal Books, 2004). This discipleship counseling tool helps Christians resolve their personal and spiritual conflicts.

Helping Others Find Freedom in Christ DVD (Regal Books, 2007). In this DVD package, Neil explains the seven Steps to Freedom and how to apply them through discipleship counseling. He explains the biblical basis for the steps and helps viewers understand the root cause of personal and spiritual problems.

Freedom in Christ (Regal Books, 2008) is a discipleship course for Sunday School classes and small groups. Includes a leader's guide, a student guide and two DVDs covering 12 lessons and the Steps to Freedom in Christ. This course is designed to enable new and stagnant believers to resolve personal and spiritual conflicts and be established alive and free in Christ.

The Daily Discipler (Regal Books, 2005). This practical systematic theology is a culmination of all of Neil's books covering the major doctrines of the Christian faith and the problems they face. It is a five-day-per-week, one-year study that will thoroughly ground believers in their faith.

Restored (e-3 Resources, 2007). This book illustrates and expands the Steps to Freedom in Christ, making it easier for an individual to process the Steps on his or her own.

Victory Over the Darkness Series

Overcoming a Negative Self-Image, with Dave Park (Regal, 2003)
Overcoming Addictive Behavior, with Mike Quarles (Regal, 2003)
Overcoming Doubt (Regal, 2004)
Overcoming Depression, with Joanne Anderson (Regal, 2004) and DVD (2007)

Bondage Breaker Series

Praying by the Power of the Spirit (Harvest House Publishers, 2003)

Finding God's Will in Spiritually Deceptive Times (Harvest House Publishers, 2003)

Finding Freedom in a Sex-Obsessed World (Harvest House Publishers, 2004)

Specialized Books

God's Power at Work in You, with Dr. Robert Saucy (Harvest House Publishers, 2001). A thorough analysis of sanctification and practical instruction on how we grow in Christ.

Released from Bondage, with Judith King and Dr. Fernando Garzon (Thomas Nelson, 2002). This book has personal accounts of defeated Christians with explanatory notes of how they resolved their conflicts and found their freedom in Christ, and how the message of Discipleship Counseling can be applied to therapy with research results.

Daily in Christ, with Joanne Anderson (Harvest House Publishers, 2000). This popular daily devotional is also being used by thousands of Internet subscribers every day.

Who I Am in Christ (Regal Books, 2001). In 36 short chapters, this book describes who you are in Christ and how He meets your deepest needs.

Freedom from Addiction, with Mike and Julia Quarles (Regal Books, 1997). Using Mike's testimony, this book explains the nature of chemical addictions and how to overcome them in Christ.

One Day at a Time, with Mike and Julia Quarles (Regal Books, 2000). This devotional helps those who struggle with addictive behaviors and explains how to discover the grace of God on a daily basis.

Freedom from Fear, with Rich Miller (Harvest House Publishers, 1999). This book explains anxiety disorders and how to overcome them.

Extreme Church Makeover, with Charles Mylander (Regal Books, 2006). This book offers guidelines and encouragement for resolving seemingly impossible corporate conflicts in the church and also provides leaders with a primary means for church growth—releasing the power of God in the church.

Experiencing Christ Together, with Dr. Charles Mylander (Regal Books, 2006.) This book explains God's divine plan for marriage and the steps that couples can take to resolve their difficulties.

Christ Centered Therapy, with Dr. Terry and Julie Zuehlke (Zondervan Publishing House, 2000). A textbook explaining the practical integration of theology and psychology for professional counselors.

Getting Anger Under Control, with Rich Miller (Harvest House Publishers, 1999). This book explains the basis for anger and how to control it.

The Biblical Guide to Alternative Medicine, with Dr. Michael Jacobson (Regal Books, 2003). This book develops a grid by which you can evaluate medical practices, and then applies the grid to the world's most recognized philosophies of medicine and health.

Breaking the Strongholds of Legalism, with Rich Miller and Paul Travis (Harvest House Publishers, 2003). An explanation of legalism and how to overcome it.

**To purchase the above material,
contact the following:**

Freedom In Christ Ministries
9051 Executive Park Drive, Suite 503
Knoxville, Tennessee 37923
phone: (866) 462-4747
email: info@ficm.org
website: www.ficm.org

E-3 Resources
317 Main Street, Suite 207
Franklin, Tennessee 37064
phone: (888) 354-9411
email: info@e3resources.org

Also visit
www.regalbooks.com

Experience the Ministry of Reconciliation

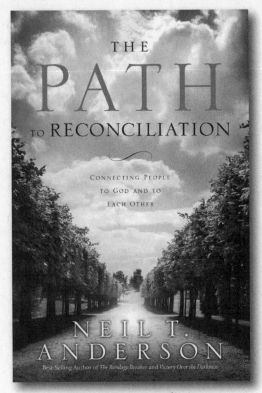

The Path to Reconciliation
Connect People to God and to Each Other
Neil T. Anderson
ISBN 978.08307.45968 • 08307.45963

We must be reconciled to God before we can be reconciled to each other. In *The Path to Reconciliation*, Neil Anderson invites us to see how Jesus brings about the supernatural transaction of reconciliation when we identify with His death, burial and resurrection. Learn how to go beyond conflict management to freedom and healing by learning the basics of reconciliation: repentance, reparation and forgiveness. Through true stories of people who have found reconciliation with God and with each other, you'll understand how to identify relationship problems, find effective solutions and guide others through the process of true reconciliation.

SMALL-GROUP BIBLE STUDY RESOURCES FROM NEIL T. ANDERSON

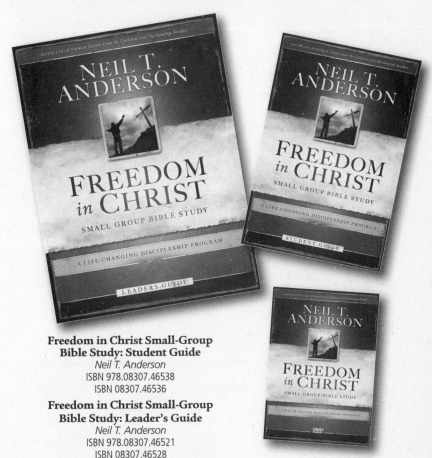

**Freedom in Christ Small-Group
Bible Study: Student Guide**
Neil T. Anderson
ISBN 978.08307.46538
ISBN 08307.46536

**Freedom in Christ Small-Group
Bible Study: Leader's Guide**
Neil T. Anderson
ISBN 978.08307.46521
ISBN 08307.46528

**Freedom in Christ Small-Group
Bible Study: 2-Disc DVD**
Neil T. Anderson
UPC 607135.014911